NINE LIVES

EXPEDITIONS TO EVEREST

ROBERT MADS ANDERSON

To my ever-so-adventurous daughter, Phoebe.

Nine Lives
Robert Mads Anderson

First published in the United Kingdom and Europe in 2020 by Vertebrate Publishing,
under licence from David Bateman Ltd – www.batemanbooks.co.nz

 VERTEBRATE PUBLISHING
Omega Court, 352 Cemetery Road, Sheffield S11 8FT, United Kingdom.
www.v-publishing.co.uk

Cover design and illustration by Ross Murray.
Book design by Cheryl Smith, Macarn Design.
Individual photography as credited.

This book is a work of non-fiction based on the life of Robert Mads Anderson. The author has
stated to the publishers that, except in such minor respects not affecting the substantial accuracy
of the work, the contents of the book are true.

A CIP catalogue record for this book is available from the British Library.

ISBN: 978-1-83981-037-4 (paperback)

Printed in Hong Kong by Asia Pacific Offset Ltd

Also by Robert Mads Anderson

7 Summits Solo

To Everest via Antarctica

Antonovs over the Arctic: Flying to the North Pole in Russian biplanes

'An amazing story capturing the essence of life's moments climbing on Everest.

'I was fortunate to share some of those moments, from my own ascent of Everest when we were in Base Camp together, to days in Lhasa waiting for flights after Robert led the ascent of the Kangshung Face.

'A remarkable read spread across nine expeditions and eighteen years of Everest life.'

Sir Christian Bonington

'Like Robert Anderson, a cat has nine lives, but doesn't write nearly as well. Robert's gripping book is required reading for both the serious climber — and for the armchair mountaineer. On a personal note, I've known and climbed with Robert for two decades. He is the real deal.'

James M. Clash
Forbes Adventure Journalist

'For two decades Robert Anderson lived and breathed Everest. He ran it out, within a whisker of the summit, on the fiendish West Ridge Direct. He led the smallest team ever to accomplish a major new route, up the gigantic Kangshung Face, getting even closer to the top. Then he chiselled away at the North Face, repeatedly, often alone. And finally he got his richly deserved summit, as leader for one of the most respected operators in the new era of commercially guided expeditions.

'Robert's story of climbing on all three sides of Everest is full of narrow escapes. But what really shines out is the canny wisdom, courage, determination and sheer fun-loving chutzpah of a defiant optimist.'

Stephen Venables
First Briton to summit Everest without oxygen

'It has never struck me before what fierce strength is required to go back and face again something that you know to be so vast, so menacing, so bated against you. You have pushed the envelope beyond mortality but the message it held has been worth it.

'I am struck by three things: the courage to go; the courage to stop; and the courage to go on again.

'You are "bloody lucky to be alive", as I was oft quoted in the press. There are hundreds of climbers all over the world who are equally bloody lucky that you lived with them through your nine lives.'

Daryl Hughes
CEO, Anderson Hughes & Partners

CONTENTS

FOREWORD

My father, Sir Edmund Hillary, wrote the foreword to Robert Anderson's book *Seven Summits Solo* in which he observed that Robert's peripatetic lifestyle was like the great wandering albatross drifting around the world. Well, nothing has changed in that regard and Robert is unquestionably one of the most travelled characters that I know. But it is when he sights a snow-capped peak that you really see a sparkle in his eyes because that is why he travels: from one great range of mountains to the next.

Climbing great mountains is a quest and Robert has dedicated his life to this journey — from 8000-metre peaks like Mt Everest, to the Seven Summits, to unknown and unnamed peaks just for the hell of it. He loves the environment of mountains, the challenge of mountains, the camaraderie built upon their flanks and the uncertainty that mountains toss into our lives.

I have known Robert since our days in the 1980s when we were all tackling unclimbed routes in the Himalayas and climbing in alpine and lightweight style with just a few other climbers and doing all the work ourselves. When you are out on the face of a Himalayan giant with no fixed ropes, no Sherpa support and no oxygen tanks, the experience is akin to being on the moon — you are on your own and you are out on a limb, a very long limb. That is the pedigree we both come from.

But as we have grown older the style of climbing has changed and for Robert it has been making lots of classic ascents, guiding and facilitating other people's climbs on the great mountains of the world. In 2018 we took a group that included my two sons, George and Alexander, to Carstensz Pyramid in the Indonesian province of Papua. Again, I saw Robert's great pleasure at being up there among the peaks, helping the members of our group attain the summits and enjoy their experiences. We attempted three of the Papuan peaks including reaching the summit of Carstensz Pyramid (4884 metres) on a beautiful day when the daily deluge remained at bay until we had returned to our tents in the valley. We attempted the east peak of Carstensz but were thwarted below the summit pyramid of the mountain by the fact that our Indonesian partners had never used crampons on the slick glacial ice before. The following day we climbed Sumantri Peak (4870 metres), which gave us a marvellous climb requiring some innovative route finding and enjoyable rock climbing on its jagged fossil-bearing limestone. Climbing over fossil bivalves, we hauled ourselves onto the summit and looked out over the jungles of northern Papua 4 kilometres below. As always, Robert was in his element.

In the spring of 2019 we took a large group of trekkers through the Khumbu Valley to Everest Base Camp. Both of our daughters were with us — Phoebe Anderson and Lily Hillary. It was their first trek into the 'high Himal', as my father used to refer to the Himalayas. And our daughters loved the trek and all the experiences along the way, and they got on like a house on fire. They were inseparable trekking companions, dancing beside the trail on the way up to EBC and literally running half the way from Gorak Shep at 5100 metres down to Lobuche at 4900 metres — our daughters had a blast. At our farewell dinner back in Kathmandu, Robert spoke about how special it had been having Phoebe with him in the Himalayas and he had tears in his eyes. And that really

INTRODUCTION

Often the first question when mountains came up in the conversation was, 'So did you climb Everest?'

'Yes,' I would say.

A pause, leaning closer, eyes more interested now. 'And what was it like then, what was the top like?'

'Absolutely wonderful. Stunning. Incredibly beautiful,' I would say.

The conversation would roll on, perhaps a few more questions, perhaps a glass of wine. Then,

'Have you ever almost died?'

Then I would pause. I would have to search for the answer.

Because there were lots of times and lots of ways I could have died and really should have died. I'd had nine expeditions to Everest. And on eight of them I had not gotten to the top. So I had gone back. Again and again. I had spent more time on obscure climbs up Everest than anyone I knew. And almost none of it was on the normal routes, or with oxygen, or with Sherpas. So the chances of dying were pretty high. Everest is a dangerous place.

The answer to the question 'Have you ever almost died?', therefore, wasn't a simple one. And it wasn't only one time when I chose to think about it. There were lots of times, sometimes multiple times, on one expedition. Even if I hadn't almost died, there was always a truism: a moment that emerged that defined that expedition.

Over the course of nine Everest expeditions, spread over eighteen years, I would change. Intense circumstances would do that to anybody. From leading an expedition that completed a new route with a team of just four people without oxygen to solo attempts on the North Face and bivouacking alone in snow holes at over 8000 metres, you learn more about the depths of yourself and others than is imaginable. Climbing Everest is more an inner journey than an outward one; it affects you right to the depth of your soul, whether you want it to or not.

As much as I would change, Everest would change. Drastically.

Seemingly eons ago, 1985, on my first expedition to Everest, Base Camp was a lonely place with only one expedition allowed per route.

In 1988, with our successful ascent of the Kangshung Face and Stephen Venables becoming the first British person to summit without oxygen in his incredible feat climbing to the top of the world, we closed out a decade that had seen Reinhold Messner's solo, the Australians' climb of White Limbo without oxygen, and Erhard Loretan and Jean Troillet's duet solo, again without oxygen, up the rarely climbed Super Couloir, in a rather unbelievable 43 hours' round trip.

By the time I was back on Everest in the early 1990s, larger commercial expeditions were just getting established. People were paying for the privilege of climbing Everest, with Rob Hall's company, now Adventure Consultants, and Scott Fisher's Mountain Madness, leading the charge.

Meanwhile I was hiding out on the more remote North Face, first with a small team, then with no team as I tried and tried again to solo the mountain at the tail end of the monsoon. I probably had more North Face time than anyone on Everest, with five attempts in as many years, and more near-death experiences than I cared to think about.

The 90s were punctuated by the 1996 disaster, recounted vividly in Jon Krakauer's book *Into Thin Air*. Suddenly Everest was more public than ever. Yet it was also still a small and private world among the guides, from knowing Rob Hall in New Zealand, to David Breashears who directed the IMAX movie *Everest*, who I'd grown up rock climbing with in Eldorado Springs, Colorado, to Pete Athans who I'd climbed with on the West Ridge of Everest on my first expedition. One day I had a postcard from Rob Hall in Everest Base Camp and the next day the press were asking for interviews to comment on his being stranded in the heights.

By 2000, commercial expeditions had pretty much overrun the mountain. And I still hadn't been to the top. Maybe my solo attempt in winter (still not completed) was a bit too far out there?

The ever astute and unforgiving Liz Hawley in Kathmandu, the doyen of Everest climbing and keeper of the Himalayan database and all things Everest, having provided long-running and quiet encouragement for my more adventurous pursuits, assured me that 'Yes, I probably had the record for most times on Everest without reaching the top.' Yet she never said 'failure', and I never felt that.

Everest is just too big, at times too fun, and too big a part of the earth to not be guaranteed an experience, often beyond belief. Sometimes sad, sometimes hard, always challenging. And fantastic experiences with climbing partners, with friends who you then know and share more mountain time with, for life.

Nine times, though. That is a lot of Everest time. Who would attempt Everest nine times before they finally summit?

And what would be of interest in those attempts? Certainly not the packing, the preparation, the logistics, the travel. I realised that on every expedition, there was a moment, a very memorable moment. And on nine expeditions at least nine lives. So here is the answer to that question, 'Have you ever nearly died?'

1

EVEREST WEST RIDGE DIRECT – LIFE IS INTUITION

The entrance to Camp 3 high on Everest's remote West Ridge Direct in Tibet was a slot cut into the ice of the slope. The only way in was to twist sideways and squeeze through, kicking unseen crampon points into the thin, icy ridge leading down into the subterranean darkness of the crevasse.

The crevasse had a thin ice roof; light snuck dimly through the doorway crack and then ran in splintered, snow-covered lines that snaked across the ceiling 5 metres above me. Nowhere was the snowy floor level; it pitched and heaved, then sloped off rapidly into a black hole behind our two tents. The nylon of the tents alternatively flopped and stretched tight above the uneven floor.

The tents should have been a haven, a place to call home, if only for one night. But the crevasse was already 'home'; we were inside. However, it was plainly evident there wasn't a home gene anywhere in this crevasse. Outside, the tents would have been warding off elements. Here, the only element was ice; it was like pitching a tent in a sealed icebox.

A draught of frozen air blew in through the door, flowed over the tents, rustled the nylon, a noise of leaves dying in the autumn, then swept off into the black hole behind us to nowhere. It was surreal: tents buried in a crevasse on a mountain. It was the darkest, most shadowed corner part of a Dr. Seuss story of my youth.

The temperature was minus 8°C (18°F), never more, never less. It didn't seem so cold at first, but the dim light, the ice walls, the flow of air, soon chilled the soul. We were here to make an attempt at life in the icebox.

Into this space, my rope-mate Randall Grandstaff and I stepped. Mid-afternoon, the haze of 7315 metres (24,000 feet) of elevation, the wind rising, the sun falling, with only enough day and energy left to get the stove going, inside the tent, inside the crevasse. The light, filtered by the crevasse, filtered by the tent, filtered by eyes seeing life through an altitude haze, created a fuzz of what should have been reality. When the stove boiled, the steam floated off it like smoke from a cremation, hazy, hanging, then catching in the wind flowing from the entrance and carrying itself off into the black hole behind us.

We had both been eating and sleeping on mountains for years. It was second nature; we needed no thought to know what we needed to do. Hanging off cliffs, sleeping in hammocks by night, balancing stoves and heating tea in the dark, we had done it all in wind and rain and snow until it was automatic. We had started young when it was all so exciting that difficulties were fun, mistakes were laughed at and we became very good at it without thinking about it. Randall hailed from, of all places, Las Vegas, Nevada, but was one of the most active of first ascensionists at the nearby climbing area, Red Rocks, putting up hundreds of difficult new routes. He was gregarious, outspoken, highly talented and had a great eye for the best way up a mountain. And he was a lot of fun to climb with, armed with both the enthusiasm and the experience to help get us up the hard leads on the West Ridge. We had been thrown together by chance, would climb hard and fast for just three days, and never climb together again. I would know a small part of who he really was, and after a rappelling accident some years later, he would die long before his time.

Our apprenticeship and confidence level in the mountains were essential because altitude added a whole litany of new challenges. Instant soup boiled steadily for ten minutes left the noodles still crunchy. The noodles got stuck in the teeth, they went sideways in the throat, they weren't nutrition in any sense of the word. Hot lemon followed that and never seemed more than lukewarm packs of sugar and flavouring, biting at the throat. Then it was time to go to sleep. Randall took out his contact lenses. I wondered why he was wearing contacts and he assured me they worked, they didn't fog. Snippets of civilised life below translated to the heights that seemed incongruous with our existence. Randall put the contacts in their case before they froze and zipped them into a small pocket in the top of his sleeping bag. Maybe they doubled as a pillow.

Then we were in our sleeping bags, the light went out of the roof, the temperature still hovered at, yes, still the same, an unmoving minus 8°C. Not so cold really, but the air outside the crevasse was not the same as the air inside. Inside it was fetid and cloying and was thick-laden with ice crystals. It preyed on us and because it had no life it was a dead weight of air. We had Everest ice below us, around us, above us.

Above 7000 metres there is no thought of sleep, not without oxygen. Maybe later we hoped, but never the first night.

Being our first time on Everest, there was the thought that 'Oh, so this is Everest, this is what it is like.'

Yet in nine more expeditions spread over eighteen years, I would never have a night anything like those two Randall and I spent at Camp 3 on Everest's West Ridge Direct. Where we knew so little and had to act intuitively with so much, just to stay alive and ultimately to get down.

That night we lay for twelve hours, drifting in and out of semi-consciousness. The cold air penetrated the down of our sleeping bags as if they were threadbare cotton sheets. The ice underneath came up through the pads in jagged lumps that pushed and prodded our skinny high-altitude bodies. The stars, the friendly stars and the connection to the heavens, were gone. It was completely, absolutely pitch-black. At least I thought so, until sometime later, in the twisting and turning of the night, I looked out the tent door and spotted a hole in the crevasse roof through which a single star showed, a single dim pinprick of light. But the earth turned and the star left and pitch-blackness was back. The crevasse was our coffin; it surrounded and covered us.

The sun never really came up; the cave just went from pitch-black to kind of black, then mostly black. Then long after time should have woken the morning up, a little grey crept into our lives. The stove was a tangled metal mass of freezing parts. The water was frozen. The lighters wouldn't spark, and the little wheels spun and tore skin from our thumbs that fell white and frozen into the ice crystal and became the same.

This was Everest, that was all it was. This was to be expected; it wasn't supposed to be easy after all. We were climbing and suffering in the footsteps of our heroes. We would persevere. Matches, plain old wooden matches, soon torched the stove, overflowing with fuel, and the fumes exploded and burst out across the tent then faded into a troubled low sputtering flame. It took an hour to melt a small bowl of ice chunks. We were climbers, we were meant to be out climbing, but any type of movement was hard.

Hardest of all was the boots, the first generation of plastic climbing boots, the shiny and new and oh so cool-looking white plastic mountaineering boots. When we had pulled them out of their boxes in our packing warehouse, we felt like we were stomping the last few steps to the top of Everest just looking at them. Now they were ice chunks, in our ice world, stuck onto our iced-up toes. Why did they have to make them white?

Lower legs and toes were wooden inside the boots, then the crampons, the strap-on crampons, almost like Ed Hillary and Tenzing Norgay wore on the first ascent. They were old-fashioned goofiness taking half an hour a side to loop around and around the foot and snug up, either so tight that an hour later they had to come off and circulation restored with a slow tide of blood coming in, with a wave of pain, or so loose the toes skidded sideways and the boot fell off them and they had to be retightened, the fingers leaving skin in the buckles, turning red and producing the headache-jarring, throbbing pain from the fingers to the hands to the wrists pain, when stuffed back in the mittens.

Slamming the crampons into the ice, and thus the toes into the front of the boots, led up the mini-ridge and out of the crevasse slice in the ice. The head popped up, looking about from side to side, surveying the scene, very groundhog like. A blast of sunshine, of wind, of air, of life rushed across us. The first step out onto the slope induced vertigo. The light on the shining snow slope, the prickly points of the crampons grabbing at the ice like twelve magnetic connections back to earth, the far, far away glacier suspended below us.

The West Ridge on Everest extends kilometres out from the mountain. So while you are climbing Everest, you are also on this immense exposed ridge that forms the border between Nepal and Tibet. It catches the wind, but it rewards with the views. Looking out, there is Pumori and Cho Oyu and Gyachung Kang and so many peaks that you could climb something new every day of the year. So on the rolling dinosaur tail of a ridge rolling down from the summit of Everest we climbed, brandishing axes and sticky, pointy boots and suits making us as big as snowmen.

We'd already put the ropes up this section, so advancing was simply a matter of putting the ascender on the rope, step up, slide, another step. Not steep, like a black ski run only, but there was no rhythm, no real sense of movement, no glory. Only cold wooden feet, leaden thoughts, air, so little air and so much wind, rushing its madness over the ridge. No climbers below surfaced from Camp 2. On the Lho La col at Camp 1, only distant black dots marked the tents. No movement could be seen. It was us and Everest. Last climbers on earth.

The ridge rolled off the right side into Nepal, down into the Khumbu Icefall, 1220 metres (4000 feet) below. This was where in 1963 Tom Hornbein and Willi Unsoeld had climbed up out of the Khumbu and onto the ridge. Out here is where the iconic shot of one lone man climbing along the ridge was taken that graces the front cover of Tom's book, *Everest: The West Ridge*, the black summit pyramid rising in the background as the clouds welled up from below. As much as the ridge was unbelievably long, we were stepping from the traditional 1953 Base Camp we had started from, onto a section of the original West Ridge route. Then, where Tom and Willi had gone left, across the North Face and out into the Hornbein Couloir, we would continue straight up along the crest of the ridge on our direct route to the summit.

The final black summit pyramid looked both touchable and unbearable, the plume streaming, the black rock sitting atop the snow. It was for dreamers and wasn't connected to our reality. Yet some part of our brains was already there. With climbers it always is, otherwise you wouldn't be there at all. There were nineteen of us on this expedition, and every one of us was dreaming and hoping and swearing somewhere inside us that we were going to stand on the top of the world. From Jim Bridwell to Bill Forrest, Jay Smith to Pete Athans, Andy Politz to Ed Webster, we had a mix of personalities whose abilities spanned the spectrum from big walls to big mountains. It must be said, none of us really knew what we were up for.

The year 1985 saw the beginning of the end of an era for Everest. The forces that would shape Everest's future were being put in place. It was the last year the Nepalese allowed only one team on each route on Everest and they soon began to reap the financial benefits that drive today's business. So while there might be a few teams in Base Camp, we were each headed up in a different direction. Base Camp was still very much a small, friendly village of fewer than 50 people, everyone knowing and interacting with everyone else.

Expeditions were still largely nationalistic, and we mirrored that, with the Norwegians on the South Col and our team, the 1985 American Expedition, on the West Ridge Direct. We weren't on our route by choice, as the Norwegians had the permit for the South Col, and our leader, Dave Saas, took what he thought was the next best option. That it was a long, torturous climb with a dangerous, loose, rocky cliff to just get to the route, a central section with a traverse of 2 kilometres at over 7000 metres and then a final 1000 metres up a steep technical rocky ridge to the summit didn't deter him.

The West Ridge Direct on Everest had first been attempted by a French team in 1974, when six died in an avalanche. Its first ascent was by a strong Yugoslavian climbing team in 1979. It had a second ascent and then has never been successfully repeated ever since. These days no one even seems to attempt it, despite it being a natural and beautiful route, one of only three prominent ridges on Everest.

Climbing teams were also still expected to really climb, so we were out in front, fixing ropes, putting in anchors and carrying our own gear. Our Sherpas were in support, carrying supplies up to our established camps. When I fixed ropes for a week above Camp 4 at 7500 metres (24,606 feet) up to our Camp 5 at 8100 metres (26,575 feet), I did all the leading and my Sherpa Lakpa climbed along behind with extra ropes, yet always encouraging me to climb faster.

We spent a fantastic week up high, climbers coming up in support of our camp, with just me and Lakpa starting early, climbing high and dropping back to the windy camp for noodles every night. By night, our tent was picked up by the wind and dropped back onto the ice with us both inside. By day, we climbed with Russian MiG aircraft oxygen masks and tanks weighing 4 kilos (9 pounds) each. We shared intense and beautiful moments of climbing on Everest high over the Tibetan Plateau, with hard snow and fractured but friendly staircased vertical rock on the ridge.

Our overall team had been built in a ramshackle fashion. Our leader Dave Saas had recruited Jim Bridwell as a climbing leader, as iconic and polarising a figure as could be found in the world of American climbing. Jim in turn had recruited his Yosemite climbing partners, hard men from the granite walls. Jim had also invited Bill Forrest, who I'd worked and climbed with in Colorado. Then Bill in turn had called me up in my far-flung post at Ogilvy advertising in New Zealand and invited me along. I accepted immediately. Who wouldn't? I was a climber and it was Everest; it seemed a completely natural thing to do.

The team was an admittedly ragtag bunch, but what we lacked in expedition experience, we made up for in enthusiasm and that incredibly rare opportunity to touch the top of the world.

Alongside us in Base Camp were the Norwegian team, attempting to become the first from their country up Everest. Led by the shipping magnate Arne Naess, he had recruited Chris Bonington to focus on logistics and organisation. Chris had yet to summit, so he had the added advantage of joining a phenomenally talented team and having his own shot at the top.

Originally slated to join the Norwegian team was my climbing partner from Romsdal, Norway, Hans Christian Doseth. I had met Hans when I'd moved to Norway, bouldering along the fjords and putting up new routes in the Romsdal Valley together. As fluid, powerful and enthusiastic as anyone I'd climbed with, Hans had subsequently visited me in the US and climbed the routes I'd grown up with in Eldorado Springs, Colorado, before going on to ascents of the big walls in Yosemite.

After living in Norway, I had returned with my climbing friend and artist Steve Sanford, for another summer climbing together while staying with Hans in Andalsnes and climbing new routes in Romsdal. A year later when Hans had already been picked for the Everest team, he went to Pakistan. There he completed a new route on Trango Towers, but so sadly died on the descent. Chris Bonington had shared the news with me as we passed through Bangkok en route to Kathmandu. Suddenly, the light-heartedness of climbing faded, I sat in my hotel room that night thinking of Han's enthusiasm, his power, the joy of climbing that had emanated from him. He didn't seem to get anywhere near nine lives, he had barely had one life and it seemed to have come and gone so quickly. It was an ominous start to our expedition.

1985 was also the year Dick Bass, having worked a deal to tag along on the Norwegian permit, came in with David Breashears and finished off the Seven Summits, creating an adventure legacy that now attracts thousands of people a year to the tallest peak on each of the seven continents. Base Camp was a place where a card game with Arne, Dick, Chris and David in the evening hours was as much a part of the experience as climbing Everest itself. There was no real competition and, even among this group of legendary personalities, very little ego. We were off on a climbing holiday, an Everest climbing holiday. With David Breashears guiding Dick Bass to the summit, people realized that Everest was within reach of people who weren't lifelong climbers.

Meanwhile, everyone on our own team were Everest virgins. As our promotional brochure stated, more Americans had been on the moon than on the top of Everest. It was still a very rarefied experience. As much as we all had read of Everest history, of Everest maladies, of Everest advice, nothing had prepared Randall and me for the realities of really living and climbing on Everest.

While the acronyms HAPE (high altitude pulmonary oedema) and HACE (high altitude cerebral oedema) were somewhere in our heads, the reality of them was a mystery. Fluid building up in our lungs or our brains just wasn't yet part of what we expected. We knew Everest would be hard, but where was the line between fatigue and not getting enough oxygen because our lungs were bubbling? When did a headache then become a crushing headache, then destroy your ability to think coherently or even walk straight?

Soon after arriving at Camp 3, Randall's and my minds began to be taken by the mountain. Our reaction was more believing that we were perhaps weak and must really toughen up. This was Everest and we needed to be strong.

Only today, right now, climbing out of Camp 3, did Randall and I realise we were going nowhere and doing it slowly. We were not being strong; we really weren't being much of anything. The dream of Everest and the reality of Everest were separated by a bodily pain that made progress impossibly slow and mentally painful. Our crampons crunched the ice and it crackled and broke underfoot in painful snaps of the ice. Heat and smells quickly rose inside the down suit, while the fingers on the axe burned as they touched metal.

There had been a toothbrush at some point, but the bristles all fell out one night in the cold so it would be a long furry month of a mouth until a new brush could be called on from Base Camp. All this Western-induced wimpiness would be exorcised later in the expedition, but, now, it was still assumed the simple comforts were needed. In reality, little of it helped one get to the top.

The only thing that gets one to the top is climbing until you get there, and too much thought about even that just gets in the way.

It was already 10.30 a.m. in the morning, the sun was blazing, the wind was rising, clouds were moving up from Nepal. It wasn't really bad weather, but it never is really good weather on the ridges of Everest, just calms between the storms. There was always an excuse for not climbing, for not reaching our objective of Camp 4 another 2 kilometres along the ridge. I guess Randall and I talked, we both knew it was hopeless, but I also knew we didn't want to give up on reaching the next camp. We weren't quitters. We were Everest climbers. We weren't going to give up on climbing higher.

Climbing was in our thickened high-altitude blood, the natural thing to do, to go up until we could go no further, and then go down. So we rationalised that we would just retreat for the day, we would hang at Camp 3, we would climb higher tomorrow. This had a sense of logic, avoiding the defeatism floating around us. So back we went, down to the crevasse, back into the hole, to 'rest', to plan, to scheme and to climb higher on Everest tomorrow.

The second coming was worse than the first. We knew what to expect. The crevasse had no romance; no light-hearted 'we are sleeping in the bowels of Everest' comments passed our lips. We beat and coerced the stove into action. It sputtered and fumed and didn't do a stove-like job at all. We gave up and dived deeper into our sleeping bags to face the night, a night blacker than the last. Blacker because I kept my eyes closed, blacker because there was no space in my head for thought, it was only black. Time was a lifetime of shivering, hard ice below, icy air above, us the ice cubes in the middle. It went on forever until the grey of morning arrived.

But even then, we didn't really move, we just muttered, we rolled over. Maybe we should just rest another day?

The grey was punctuated by Jay Smith's arrival, having stomped up the hill from Camp 2, to climb to Camp 4 with us. He edged down into the crevasse, he tried to make light conversation, he quickly saw we weren't really up to climbing higher on Everest that day. We were zombies.

I put on my climbing suit, I put on my boots, I put on my pack. That took me an hour. Then Jay and I helped Randall put his boots on and lace them up. Randall was fun, he was joking, but he really wasn't making sense. But I wasn't that good a judge. Yes, I could dress myself, but only barely and it was a lot of work.

Jay was looking at us intently. He'd figured out we weren't really well. I finally fitted my crampons and pointed them up and out of the hole. Surfacing, the air and the sun were twice as intense as the previous day, as if we had become cave dwellers. I looked up; I took a few steps in the upward direction. The lethargy was something I'd never experienced before, the inability to physically move forward, to control my mind and get my body moving.

A step, then a stand there, a look at the view, a look around some more. Maybe a story would start in my head. Then more breathing, then an 'Oh yeah, I'm climbing, I should take a step.' Then some thought about what that step might take, the work it would entail. My mind fighting against itself. I was going nowhere. I certainly wasn't going up to Camp 4.

I turned and started down the ropes. It was now a down day, even under an intensely blue sky. Clip the carabiner into the rope, careful but clown-like steps, bringing the legs under control, feeling the ease and speed of down while still a fatigue, a muscle lethargy, pervaded. Crampons give your feet no play; there is no slipping or sliding. Those twelve points go into hard snow and that is where they stay. And movement, torqueing or slide are all taken up by the foot in the boot, and in a hard plastic boot that isn't much. So the movement ricochets up into your leg, twisting and turning until the muscles calm most of it down, but sometimes the twist goes right up into your spine and reaches up and gives your head a good shake, shaking it on its stem. With the inevitable high-altitude headache already, that is an unfriendly sensation.

Randall came out of the cave and I looked back up at him, set large against the sky and the ridge above. He took one normal step, then one very big step, then one wild, drunken swinging sideways spinning step and flew face first into the snow. Oh no. What to do?

Jay helped Randall up. He repeated his performance. Then again, but with a few extra steps in between. They came up to me.

'We just need to get him down,' said Jay. 'Keep going.'

I went. I felt like a strange stick man, but my body was obeying commands. Randall's body was doing none of the sort. We kept going, me in front, Randall in the middle, Jay bringing up the rear, clipping Randall though the anchors. We traversed across the moonscape of sliding ice slabs and sun cups, dished-out ice pockets and snowy drifts, snow going to ice, to sugar, to powder, all in one foot. We moved, we stopped, we yelled back and forth, we moved again.

We stepped onto the ledge outside the snow cave that was Camp 2. I don't remember either reaching it or passing it, but we did as it was on the way and that is what altitude does. Then we dropped off into the steep snow gullies leading to the rock cliffs. This part of the wall I'd climbed with Randall a week previously, swapping leads as we led up through rock and ice bands, escaping the steep ground below and eventually breaking into the upper slopes. I'd led one steep pitch up through the stacked blocks, rocks set like shaky library books atop each other, and then I'd belayed Randall as he led up an even steeper rock band, climbing out over an overhang of rock at 6553 metres (21,500 feet) that would have been challenging at sea level. Randall had gone up into the cliff and stemmed his legs out and climbed through it in a single 100-metre (328-foot) lead that took us up out of the cliffs and into the broad snow slopes above, opening the way to the upper ridge.

Now we just had to rappel down through this, down the cliff and then into the 457 metres (1500 feet) of gully and then the ice face and we'd be back to the reassuring horizontal, air-rich plateau of the Lho La, where we had our Camp 2.

The ropes tightened up in the steep sections, making it hard to transition from anchor to anchor. It was so steep the ropes swung free over the rock cliffs. At the anchors I could lean in and the ice was right in front of me; it was climbing a big wall on Everest with no horizontal relief.

It was hard to help Randall on the rappels; Jay just had to send him off and I would watch below, ready to pull the rope tight and slow his rappel and then catch him to make sure he didn't unclip from the rope. Then I'd take off again and Jay would slide down to transition anchors for Randall and send him off to me. I wasn't really being much help; it was more of a false crutch. When I went first, at least the ropes were straight to the next anchor. I reassured myself that it was some help. And that if Randall did fall, I could tighten up enough on the rope to slow his descent. I knew Jay was doing the hard work. Jay was tough; he taught and guided for the US Navy SEALs, and this was just Everest.

Steep ice gullies curved away and then spread out into broad swathes of ice once we descended over the largest of the rock cliffs. I reached the end of the first rappel over the cliffs leading into them and stepped sideways onto a footstep of ice that had been cut into the slope. It held a half of a fat high-altitude boot. The anchor above disappeared into the snow, and there was no real way to tell what it was, but one advantage of being on Everest with a bunch of Yosemite big-wall climbers is you could pretty much trust they all knew how to put in anchors. I looked up and saw Randall start down through the cliff bands above.

As we'd gotten lower, Randall's feet had started to descend in a more mannerly fashion. They weren't really under control, but moving downward, or maybe the vertical, direct nature of the rappels gave him little choice but to move straight down, one foot falling naturally below the other.

I hung on the anchor 100 metres below him as he started through the rock bands. His feet splayed wide high above me, then he suddenly pitched sideways, his feet crashing about on the cliff, crampons grating and crashing against the rock. At first I was worried he was falling down the rope and so I pulled it tighter. Then the rocks below him caved in and started falling away, rattling and cracking over the bottom of the cliff before falling free onto the ice and tumbling into the ice gully leading to my stance.

The rocks were part of an outcrop composed of blocks set upon blocks, and when the lower ones were kicked the entire tower suddenly plummeted down. They didn't start slowly; they didn't topple or need time to gather speed. They just cut loose and went from being part of Everest to flying down, hailing out of the sky straight towards me.

I leapt sideways, tugging the rope even tighter. There was just enough rope at the anchor for me to pull myself off to the right of a thin ridge as the rocks flew towards me.

Rocks shooting overhead sound like missiles, hard edges catching and spinning and whistling in the air as they fall. They were big, head-sized and bowling-ball, rolling and sharp and spiky, shooting past. A few small ones hit my jacket; bigger ones crashed into my pack. It was a whole garden full of rocks cut loose and sprouting and tumbling down the ice, over me, around me, into me. Then they rushed off down the gully, following on their merry way, before disappearing in puffs of rock and ice dust another half a kilometre below.

I hung twisted sideways and pushed out on the ropes, pulled as far off around the little ridge as I could, front points pushing out from the lone foothold, the other foot stemmed out on the ice to the side as far from the direct path as I had been able to reach. Death had roared down, missed and carried on its way. No noise was left behind, no revelation, just simple knowledge that if I hadn't leapt to the far side of the ledge, the bigger rocks and main mass would have hit me, and that would have been it. No drama, no fear, nothing to think about, just dying very quickly and simply and silently as that.

I eased myself back over onto the ice slope. Around me, grooves and minefields and furrows cut the ice where the swathe of rocks had cut into the ledge where I had been standing before I'd jumped sideways. Everything had been hit except me. The ice ledge was shattered and had gone down the mountain in a puff of air, dissolved off the mountain. The smell, the peculiar smell of rock hitting rock, a smoke-like essence hung in the air. I was shaking, but only a bit. It was still a long way down. It wasn't about fear, it was simply about getting through it, then carrying on. Randall rappelled down to the anchor and I clipped him in.

We were out of the rock cliffs, and the ice was unlikely to break free; just one long rappel after another now with too-tight ropes, tiny steps, endless clipping and unclipping of the rope, always the rope, the connection back to earth leading us down. There really wasn't much to think about, just the line leading us down, the slide, the feet, fatigue, the deep breathing for no reason except there was no air.

We would get back to the base of the ice eventually, but for now it was just good not to have been taken out by the rocks. It was all that simple. We'd gotten up because we loved to climb, I'd gotten down because I didn't pause to think, just act. After all, it was Everest; it was all to be expected.

A month later, Jay Smith and I stuttered to a halt in the Grey Band at 8600 metres (28,200 feet) on the West Ridge Direct. Oxygen problems, cylinders hissing air uselessly, vertical climbing on frayed ropes, brought us to a point where going up may have gained us the summit, but getting down again wasn't at all likely. Jay had more oxygen, he may have made it, but we decided to go down together. It would be five years before Jay and I would be back to climb together on Everest again.

After my return to flat ground from the expedition, I had no real sense of what was next, but I knew I wanted to go back to Everest. We had not made it because we really didn't know what we were doing. The climbing I had done up high with Sherpa Lakpa had been some of the most fun I'd ever had in the mountains. There was nothing as good as climbing on Everest. And sometimes nothing as bad I had to admit. I'd had the chance to see what a successful expedition really looked like. Arne Naess's strong lead-from-the-front style on his Norwegian Expedition, the funding he had and how he had managed his team made them one of the most successful expeditions ever, summiting in the end of April before the mountain even warmed up. Being Norwegian certainly didn't hurt in the cold conditions and they were the most successful expedition to date, with seventeen people on top.

I'd also had the chance to look over Chris Bonington's shoulder at his new Apple computer as he took me through the lists and charts he put together to orchestrate a smooth ascent that put them on the summit so efficiently. Anyone who has taken the time to read Bonington's book, *Everest South West Face*, and worked their way all the way through to the appendix, would have seen his chart movement spreadsheets and his projected versus actual ascents. They were a work of art to me. An expedition could be a freewheeling mix of climbing partners, ice axes and food stashes carried up and stashed in small tents. But to be successful it also had to be meticulously planned and well-funded so you could arrive on the mountain and then execute the plan. That was the key to really putting together a successful Everest expedition, long before the climbing ever started.

I'd also noted David Breashears' climb to the top with Dick Bass in their minimalist two-man team that seemed to simply scamper unencumbered up the mountain. They skipped Camp 3 and climbed unroped from the South Col. If you were climbing from the South Col, that was certainly a good way to do it.

Climbing high on the mountain, with Andy Politz, who reached over 8000 metres at Camp 5 without oxygen, I'd seen how a bit more determination could get you a whole lot higher than you might think. Then climbing with Pete Athans above Camp 5 on our first summit attempt, in the dark vertical couloir leading up to the Grey Band, just how hard climbing was still possible at high altitude, notwithstanding down suits, big boots and heavy antiquated oxygen systems.

While I had first met Ed Webster in our rock-climbing days years before in Arizona, it would be the friendship we formed on Everest in 1985, continued with a new route on the Diamond in Colorado in 1986, and then meeting again the following year in Beijing that would form the core of our climbing team on the Kangshung Face when I returned to Everest.

I was working in New Zealand, had just started my own advertising agency with my partner Daryl Hughes in Auckland, yet thoughts of Everest still filled my head. We had made so many beginners' mistakes on the West Ridge Direct. From how we funded it, to the equipment we had, to the members of the team. All the basics were wrong. It wasn't like we should have known better, but it seemed like there could be a good climb to be done on Everest if I just worked it out and led it myself. I liked to do first ascents and new climbs that were challenging. Everest by an established route, with a big team, and using oxygen didn't have that appeal any more. I pored over maps and Everest history.

I liked the idea of Tibet, it seemed remote and wild and adventurous just to go there. The North Face was very interesting, but then I started looking at the East Face, the really remote Kangshung Face. Only one climb of it ever made. And it was huge, the biggest face on the mountain. What could be more challenging, more exciting than a new route up the biggest face on Everest? And I didn't want a whole host of people, of climbers who weren't the best. All I wanted was a small team of the best climbers in the world. And, certainly, no oxygen. I felt oxygen was cheating, was just making Everest easier and taking away the biggest part of the challenge. Why take the tallest mountain in the world and make it shorter?

Corresponding back and forth to the Chinese Mountaineering Association (CMA) was so slow and I didn't think they were taking me seriously. So following a business meeting in Sydney, Australia, I flew up to Beijing. I met with the Director of the CMA, Ying Dao Shui. We drank jasmine tea and talked Chinese mountaineering, yaks and rules.

Lots of rules. And money, lots of money. But we formed a grudging respect and eventually a friendship that would serve me well over my next decade of climbing in Tibet. On my fourth day in Beijing we were pretty much done. I had a permit for the whole of the Kangshung Face, any route I wanted. I had a liaison officer and an interpreter, I had dates set and I had yaks, 60 yaks. We went out for the day, with Mr Ying, our driver, and an interpreter, who was just along for the ride. We visited and chanted at monasteries and finished up with Peking Duck and Maotai in a banquet hall where I was the only Westerner among hundreds of people. The next day I had my official permit.

Ed Webster showed up in Beijing that day, having accompanied Roger Marshall on his solo attempt on the North Face of Everest. Ed had taken the opportunity to solo a new route on Changtse and was buzzing with energy.

'What are you doing here, Robert? Why are you in Beijing?'

I showed him my permit. 'This is it,' I said. 'This is what I wanted. My own Everest permit, the side of the mountain where no one goes.'

'Can I go?' Ed asked, full of expectation.

It seemed serendipitous, climbing on the West Ridge together with Ed and now meeting in Beijing, and it seemed he should go along. And he desperately wanted to go I could tell, even when I outlined my plans.

For my climbing team, I wanted them all to want to summit fiercely. And I had to feel they too could climb Everest by a new route without oxygen. That was it. I didn't expect them to raise money; I could do that. I just wanted them to be able to climb hard stuff and go high without oxygen. And to do that they would need to want it very badly.

Ed and I had climbed in Colorado together after Everest, doing a new route on the Diamond. Ed had the talent to find and do new routes, a whole different challenge in climbing. You don't have a guidebook, or something or someone to follow. You don't know how hard it might be.

You have to look at the mountain, you have to be able to read it, you have to know what it will take to get up, picking a way that makes sense and is as safe as it can be. Very few climbers had that decision-making ability. It was much more art than science. It was the most challenging and exciting part about climbing.

The not knowing, the discovery, and then finding a passage.

Doing new routes was a whole, much bigger world before you ever challenged yourself physically. It was the purest form of the art of climbing. I'd completed a host of new routes, starting with a few in Colorado and then many in Norway. Ed had climbed in the north-east, the desert and in the remote Black Canyon of the Gunnison National Park. He had the mindset to make countless decisions regarding route and gear that we would need to make over and over on something as big as Everest. And he could really climb. I had seen that on the Diamond on our new route — he had the natural dedication and talent needed to get up something never done before, in good style. And now we had both been to Everest, we were tested on the heights and knew what it was like. He was my first teammate.

When I got back from Beijing I talked to Jay Smith. We had been up high on the West Ridge Direct, and his level of experience on new routes was immense, on ice and snow and rock. He wasn't interested in being well known; he was interested in climbing — it was all he really seemed to do. But Everest had been too much sitting around for him, and even though we had done some good climbing, it was as he repeated, 'two weeks climbing crammed into two months'. 'But I have a friend, he can really climb. You should talk to Paul Teare.'

Coming from Jay, no one got a higher recommendation. So Paul came out for a visit to Colorado on one of my sojourns home. He was witty, taciturn, talented and egoless. His list of climbs was incredible and on a good day with good ice he would sneak off into Yosemite Valley and quietly solo the routes that scared most of us to death even with a rope on. He had done big new routes with Jay in Alaska and Canada. Now there were three.

Living in New Zealand, I felt too far removed from the centre of commerce and the sponsors I wanted to talk to were primarily in the

US, so I'd hired a public relations director in New York City to help me with fundraising, Wendy Davis.

'Robert, we need something to actually talk about, something new to say. This Kangshung Face, people can't even pronounce it. It's the thirty-fifth anniversary of the Everest first ascent, how about something around that?' It wasn't actually the catchiest of anniversaries, but it was a start.

Wendy tracked down Sir John Hunt in London, expedition leader of the first successful Everest expedition in 1953, and called me:

'Okay Robert, he wants to see you. Don't screw this up.'

What does one say to a Knight Bachelor? How does one address him? My American upbringing hadn't prepared me for this. I went to London to find out.

A minute after meeting him he said, 'Just call me John.' That was easy. And after a slow and rather uncomfortable cup of tea, John said, 'I don't have to be back to the House of Lords until four o'clock. Perhaps we should move to the bar for a pint.'

We retired to the bar. We talked climbing, we talked logistics. I was no longer sitting with a knight and baron but with a talented climber who had carried gear above the South Col for Hillary and Tenzing's ascent. John had stepped in and taken over leadership of a disparate and opinionated team with nothing but strong personalities. He was perhaps one of the few people on earth who had looked down the East Face from the South Col.

Emotionally, John's support gave me far more confidence than I had had before. He had led the first successful expedition to Everest and now he was lending his support to ours after meeting me and hearing of our plans. He had a level of deep experience and then the personal input that would help shape our approach and our team. He wrote me a letter following our meeting, a mix of enthusiasm, diplomacy, advice and support, that read:

My dear Robert,

It was a great pleasure to meet you yesterday and to hear more about your plans for Everest '88, as well as learning about the promotional background to the expedition. I feel honoured to be associated with the project and I am sure that my teammates of the 1953 expedition will be delighted to know that you wish to celebrate our first ascent of the mountain.

In view of the fact that ours was a British Expedition, I venture to suggest that, if it is not too late, you might invite one or two of our leading British mountaineers to join your team; I will do my best to recommend a few and will let you know.

I am glad that your own plans will be imbued with the same spirit of adventure with which we were motivated 35 years ago. We succeeded because we were such a united team and I feel sure that your own success will depend on this vital need.

I am sorry that it will not be possible for me to join you, but please know that I will be following your progress with great interest. Please keep me posted from time to time.

With every possible good wish,
John Hunt

He had added some notes in a postscript on potential team members, with a final line that would drastically change someone's life:

'Steve Venables would be my choice!'

I had a team meeting and sponsorship events planned in New York and invited Stephen over to meet our fledgling team.

Back in New York, Wendy Davis was an endless whirl of energy and enthusiasm, full of ideas, press connections and contacts. With my business connections and clients, my work with Ogilvy and in particular their group CEO and avid outdoorsman Bill Phillips, I could get Wendy in to see the executives that understood a good challenge and had the power and the access to the funding we needed. She pounded the streets and knocked on doors and by the time I showed up in New York, she had meetings set up with a host of potential sponsors, ensuring we climbers could buy the gear we needed and not worry about money.

I went out to JFK Airport to pick up Stephen, it being his first time in the Big Apple. I will always remember recognising him immediately in the throngs of people by his confident stride, his climber's rucksack, his sense of energy. I didn't even have to speak to him. I felt he would be right for our team just by the way he strode so enthusiastically across the earth.

When I flew back from New York, we had the climbing team in place: Ed Webster, Paul Teare, Stephen Venables and me. We had Wendy coordinating a great line-up of sponsors, from American Express to Rolex. We had a professional photographer who had trained with Ansel Adams in Yosemite, Joseph Blackburn. Our food selection, ever a topic of interest, would be honed, refined and perfected by Rob Dorival. Medical student Miriam Zieman would join us to be what I commonly referred to as our doctor, fully qualified or not. I'd met Mimi on our walk out from Everest two years before, and while still a student, she had the talents and sensibility to deal with our eclectic team, as well as undoubtedly the more difficult task of putting up with me as her partner. With Miklos Pinther, the chief cartographer, preparing our maps, and Norbu Tenzing, eldest son of Tenzing Norgay, in support, I could feel confident that as crazy as my plan was to climb a new route on the Kangshung Face, without oxygen and with just four people, they were absolutely the best people possible.

In my first expedition to Everest, only my intuition had saved me when the rocks came down on me.

I took that intuition to fuel the inspiration for a new route on Everest, to choose a team and set off for the remote Kangshung Face. After all, I had only really used up one life on Everest so far. I had plenty to go.

2

EVEREST KANGSHUNG FACE – LIFE IS NOW

My last night on Everest Kangshung Face, alone.

Ropes above leading up, on a jack-in-the-beanstalk climb to the top of the world.

I had been there, or nearly there, reaching the South Summit of Everest at 8749 metres (28,704 feet) four days before. Now we were going down. Only I was no longer part of the 'we'. It was the me, only the me.

I was in a hole in the snow I'd dug with my thin gloves, because I'd lent my big mittens to Stephen Venables two days before when he had lost his gloves in the avalanche. The snow hole wasn't really a hole, it was only a psychological place to lie that was a bit dished out, so I could feign sleeping without simply sliding off down the hill.

Overall, it was still better than living inside a crevasse as I had been with Randall on the West Ridge.

For nine days we'd been on the Kangshung Face on our summit bid. With Paul Teare and Ed Webster and Stephen Venables to start. We did a day up the refreshingly steep and now ever so familiar ropes we'd fixed from Advanced Base Camp to Camp 1 at 6400 metres (20,992 feet). Then a day that started in the morning dark and ended in the evening dusk at Camp 2. Then another day of fourteen hours of new climbing up our new route to the South Col. We had no Sherpas along and were carrying all our own stuff: all those tents, stoves, food, pads and sleeping bags that make for a home. None of this up and down, back and forth, carrying loads. We just put it all in the pack and off we stomped to the South Col. The packs were heavy, very heavy. We reassured ourselves we were Everest climbers, real Everest climbers. We hefted the loads and clambered up the final steep step to the South Col, the first people to ever reach the South Col from the east side. I remembered when I had first met John Hunt in London and he'd said, 'Yes, Robert, I looked over there. I went out to the edge of the Col and looked down in '53. It is a very long way down, and I'm glad we didn't have to come up that way.'

The wind was roaring across the Col as it always seems to do every afternoon without fail. The only way to pitch the tents was to get inside, flop on the ground to hold them down and have the other person stake it out, then push the poles up to get it pitched. Stephen was silhouetted inside the balloon of the tent as he battled alone inside it, and Ed grabbed the corners and staked the whole flapping mass to the ground. It was our first time to the South Col and its reputation as the world's worst camping spot was being boldly borne out.

Paul was awake all night in the tent with me, then brazenly bolted back down the route at dawn with cerebral oedema creeping up into his brain. He talked with Stephen and Ed; we all knew someone needed to go down with him. But we were already a bit addled from the altitude and we were not moving or thinking very quickly. Paul had pulled off some of our hardest leads coming up the Kangshung Face, running out our 100-metre ropes up vertical sections of blue ice. I'd seconded him on a rock pitch where for protection he picked up rocks and stuck a piton underneath and then set it down again. I cleaned the pitch by just throwing the rocks off the mountain behind us. It was some beautiful climbing done on some very non-beautiful rock and ice.

While Stephen, Ed and I played with the stoves and rolled from side to side in our sleeping bags, Paul got dressed and made the decision for us. He didn't want any of us to have to go down with him. After a quick conversation, he was off before any of the rest of us had time to even put on our boots. He was out of camp with a quickly shouted 'Make me proud. Just get to the top, okay,' and a wave. A fast and wise decision to go down. He would be back in Advanced Base Camp in seven short hours. And then there were three of us.

We wiled the day away with the ever so reticent stoves and rose at 9 p.m. to take off for the summit at 11.30 p.m. Stephen, as ever, was enthusiastically driving our timetable. As he recently reminded me, 'This is no poncey California climbing holiday.' Ed, Paul and I had spent too much time hanging out on Yosemite big walls and were certainly not alpine trained to proper Himalayan start times.

I wandered off across the South Col in the dark and in a haze. We didn't really know the way up from the South Col. How hard could it be after doing the Kangshung? So we also had a new direct start route, beginning up a cliff with a bit of scrambling, then crossed over the normal route and headed out left towards the slopes leading up to the south-east ridge. The snow varied from ankle to knee deep. After the climbing below, even though we weren't roped and there was no trail and not a soul in sight, it was very comfortable climbing, just moving up the mountain.

At dawn, the sun crept as slow as the earth turns up out of the sky behind Kanchenjunga, the world's third-highest peak, then illuminated Makalu, number five on the list of the world's big mountains. We were surrounded by giants. Then the sun was finally up and we could pretend it was warmer, although it certainly didn't feel that way. In 8000-metre cold without oxygen, your blood is not moving anyway. The snow was deep, and Stephen had thankfully moved to the front to break trail. He would be out in front all day, something he sometimes humbly fails to mention.

I'd encouraged us all not to carry packs; what was there to carry anyway? We had water bottles in our jacket pockets which soon froze.

When we hit the ridge, Stephen was already headed up the clear-cut snow crest high above. Ed was just in front of me, then paused and suddenly started down. Clouds rose and fell around us, dreamlike, still moving, but seemingly more connected to an ethereal sky above than the earth now so far below.

Ed passed me headed down. 'It's late, it's time, 4 p.m.,' he said. 'Going down.' And he quickly turned and disappeared into the rising clouds.

I definitely wasn't going down. As much as I probably should have had a turnaround time, I was climbing Everest and my turnaround was the top. I knew I wasn't exactly moving fast, but what was fast up here anyway? The snow steepened below the South Summit. The only rope we had seen since the South Col was draped down and fluttered on the snow, a shoelace of no use. With no harness (too heavy, what are they for anyway?), it was of no concern and the slope was still gentle. We had trailed a rope for a while and then left it behind. The climbing wasn't that hard and soloing up from the Col was just a lot easier. Lhotse was hazy and below me, just another one of the many peaks fading away beneath the clouds. The fact Lhotse was the fourth-highest mountain in the world didn't really register; it was way down there. We were higher than anyone else in the world.

At 5 p.m. I came to a halt at the South Summit, unable to see anything. I was immersed in the clouds and the mist and couldn't tell up from down. I'd gotten up over and onto the mini-flats of the South Summit and then the clouds all closed in around me. I circled, became confused, sat down to wait it out, and finally through the mist saw the way down. The climb had been filled with these moments, stop-frame photography moments. They were imprinted in a way that was so full of the sense of the present that what had gone before and what had gone after simply didn't exist.

The lack of food, water, air and endless physical exertion, coupled with climbing unroped up from the South Col, created a very real, but disconnected, reality. Down measured in vertical kilometres is a long way down, with the Kangshung Face extending 4000 metres (13,123 feet) vertically from Base Camp to the summit of Everest.

Stephen was on ahead above me somewhere. Ed had started down already, moving quickly and confidently down the slope. I couldn't see him in the clouds wreathing up around me. In the back of my mind, I thought I could go down to the South Col, have another rest and come back up again. I knew I couldn't get across to the top right now because I couldn't see it. I could barely see my feet.

Maybe I was lucky, even very lucky; maybe if I could have seen the top, I would have gone out there and, like others, still be sitting there today. I certainly wouldn't have been the first, or the last, to make that mistake.

I've never regretted not making that final journey then, because I'm convinced that I wouldn't have made it back. I'd have pushed my luck past what is allowed for a single life and used up all those nine lives in one, an easy thing to do on Everest. I could well have made it up to the top, but not down. I descended into the mist and caught up with Ed on the ridge above the Balcony.

'Seen Stephen?'

'No,' I answered.

And we followed our up-footprints down into the gullies below the Balcony. The clouds had broken below and it was obviously just a straight shot down to the South Col. Dark crept across the Himalayas. It started slow and built quickly. The purple was a deep purple, the pink radiant, the colours distinctive enough to paint themselves inside your head and never be forgotten.

A tent, tilted, hanging on for dear life, appeared below and we reached it as darkness set in. We had passed the tent on the way up, a lone Japanese outpost that was unused and stood ghostlike on a tiny pinnacle. We could have carried on — we should have carried on down to the South Col. But we were tired, oh so tired, and a little bivouacking seemed to make sense.

Sleeping bag-less, stove-less, water-less and food-less we sat side by side, leaning against each other. Later I curled up on the floor, but without pads it was an icy bed, so in the end we sat there shivering among some Japanese crackers and chocolate wrappers for ten hours.

I think I may have even slept a little; hard to know. As soon as a hint of light tinged the sky, I was out of the tent, looking up, for Stephen.

Where was that boy?

We were worried. But the surreal weirdness of Everest wasn't sending grim tidings. Life, death, afterlife, after deaths: all are on the same plain very high in the sky. And dying seems to send tidings to friends. None of that was happening.

Where was he? Far above me, I suddenly caught sight of Stephen. He was an indistinct figure at first, almost ghostlike, moving incredibly slowly. Then he came closer and we could see him walking, rolling and occasionally tumbling towards us, like a kid in a snowsuit. We were very happy to see him. Ed gave him the rest of his frozen water to show him how happy we were. Ed took photos, as close to a summit photo as Stephen would have of himself. Stephen had just become the first British man to summit Everest without oxygen. We really didn't think about that at the time, we were just happy we were all back together. Then we all climbed down to the South Col together.

Ed took another photo of Stephen and me leaning against each other. It was my equivalent of the summit, with expedition leader and summiteer together after a successful expedition. Except it wasn't after, it was really only the beginning, the very beginning of our attempts at staying alive over the next four days.

While I've only given this chapter one of my lives, in reality I was about to use up many of them, with day after day after day of miracles, near misses and, finally, the escape, surprisingly alive, from Everest.

We 'rested' on the South Col that afternoon and evening. Stephen and Ed's stove had run out of fuel. Mine was sputtering, I couldn't even make myself a brew. It was now our fourth night at the South Col or above without oxygen. We really should have been dead soon. We were testing the limits of the death zone. But we weren't dead at all. We still had serious conversations followed by a laugh. We obviously weren't well. I slept alone in one tent, Stephen and Ed in the other. I heard them talking during the night, like neighbouring shadows, as the wind howled over the Col.

In the morning Ed and Stephen called out for drinks, but my stove wasn't obliging. It was a struggle. I would sit up, and then I would kind of topple over, baby-like. I did want to help, I really did, I reassured myself, it was just that movement was impossible. My lighter, in trying to get the stove going, had shredded my fingers. They were freezing and half numb.

Then it was later in the day, it was 2 p.m., but we felt the way down would be quick, going down always was. So late in the afternoon we straggled over to the top of the Kangshung Face and looked down at something like 3000-plus vertical metres (9842 feet) and the kilometres of horizontal between us and our Advanced Base Camp.

Ed went off in front and had climbed down carefully along the side of the rocks to the left where we had ascended. That seemed very slow to me. We had talked about glissading, it seemed like a good idea. Might as well get on with it.

I leapt off the Col, rapidly accelerated to 100 kilometres per hour, hit rocks, flipped over and an avalanche cut loose underneath me. I felt myself being lifted up and cartwheeled down the steep slope. Feet in the snow, then hands outstretched over my head as I went sideways, up and over and came down on my feet again, the avalanche carrying me along. The avalanche went on and on, then slowly roared off below me and I came back to earth standing upright in a heap of snow. My body was racked, strung out from the tumbling. It had been like riding in a dryer with a pile of snow and ice. I was amazed I was in one piece. Just standing there perfectly balanced in the middle of this immense slope, the curve of the South Col now far above me and the kilometres of Kangshung Face rolling away below me.

Worst of all, I quickly realised I had lost my ice axe. But I always carried a back-up, a short tool in a holster. I reached for it and it was gone too. A mountaineer without an ice axe on Everest might as well be naked. Or dead. I didn't have time to feel relief at living through the avalanche because now I was at 7700 metres (25,500 feet) on Everest's largest face without an ice axe. I knew I was in big trouble. I looked up and saw Stephen silhouetted on the South Col above.

'No, no,' I yelled, 'don't glissade.' It may have been more of a croak.

How could he be so foolish, I thought, how could he not see I'd descended 150 metres (492 feet) in five seconds in an avalanche. But he hadn't seen my fall. He'd just stepped over to the edge of the Col. All Stephen could see was me waving far below him, probably viewed as enthusiasm for making such a quick glissade.

So he leapt off too, slid into the cliffs, lost control and zoomed towards me, ice axe flying away, snow shooting up behind him. His crampons caught as mine had and flipped him over and over before he too came to an abrupt halt in the snow above me.

Oh no.

He started making his way across the slope to me. It was pretty steep; the snow was avalanche runnels and ice blocks and led down into a big hole. Not something from which you would want to slide off.

'I lost my ice axe. Can I borrow one of yours?'

It could have been me asking Stephen, but it wasn't. It was him asking me. We now had a big shared problem. We traversed the slope to Ed, dipping our hands in the snow for balance. We had been climbing so long that balancing across the steep slope was second nature. And it wasn't like we had a choice.

Ed was incredulous to see me, having watched me disappear inside the avalanche and thinking I'd gone down the face with it. Stephen he'd been able to see, but I'd stopped a bit lower, behind a snowy outcrop, and appeared to have simply gone from the mountain until I reappeared with Stephen. Maybe that counted as my next life, maybe not — let's hope not, as we had a very long way to go.

Ed undid his ski pole and left it in the snow for me. I snapped it in half and Stephen and I each took a piece. This gave us something to stick in the snow anyway; it was calming, if not exactly effective.

We soon discovered the way down wasn't all that easy. It was mid-May; we had summited on the 12th and it felt like the monsoon was already starting. Every afternoon had dumped seemingly another 30 centimetres (1 foot) of snow. In the four days we had been up high, the face had loaded up so heavily that the snow now reached our knees or higher. It was like wading through wet flour, even going downhill.

We had left the South Col at 2 p.m. We crawled onto the flat ledge of our Camp 2 well after dark. It was a camp in name only, though. We'd left the tents at the South Col, thinking we would be down in a day. And I'd left the rope, as we hadn't used it up high, it was heavy, our escape should take little more than a day I was sure and it just didn't seem important, not even entering my mind. We had a stove, but it didn't really work, and we had no patience left for it. We were entering our fifth night with virtually no food, only a few sips of water, and now we had sleeping bags but no tent to sleep in.

We faced a night completely out in the open at 7400 metres (24,278 feet). But then again, we'd all bivouacked without our sleeping bags at over 8000 metres above the South Col, so maybe this wasn't so bad? With Camp 2 under a snow formation we called the Flying Wing, a huge snow abutment that extended out over our heads for 5 metres, we were completely sheltered from above. It was nature's finest tent, with a view down over the Face and over the Kama Valley, curving out and into the clouds of Tibet. It was truly beautiful.

I took off my boots, I lay in my bag, I shivered. There were stars, millions of stars. But on the Kangshung Face of Everest there is no sign of humanity, no lights below and no twinkling villages. We had seen no one beyond our own teammates for six weeks, even at Base Camp. I'd been planning this expedition in my head since I'd descended from the West Ridge and thought over all the things I had changed.

Our four-man team. That had certainly worked. No oxygen — we all seemed to still be moving anyway. Yes, of course it had been a hard route, but what fun we had. It was all the challenges real climbers looked for. And it was Everest. I'd read and followed Messner's climbs, his first ascent of Everest without oxygen in 1978 and then his solo of the North Face in 1980. I thought about what I had put in place right from the start, and, somewhat miraculously, most of it had worked. I had been quoted in the press as saying using oxygen was cheating. And we had done it. I was young and a purist, with an ego to match it seems.

As I lay on the ledge at Camp 2, I did know all these incremental successes and our summit could go away very quickly. It would all disappear if we simply froze to death that night. But I voiced none of this, as it would have involved talking and discussing and perhaps some gnashing of teeth. Better to just pass out in a fatigued stupor clutching a half water bottle full of ice chunks and hoping it would melt into a trickle of water by morning.

At dawn the sun leapt out of the horizon and melted the cold from our bodies. We went from shivering and miserable to limpid pools of humanity, lying in the heat, and soon were as hot in the baking sun as the cold of night had been. But now we knew it should be quick to get down. So we tinkered with the stove, Stephen got it going, filled half a pot with precious boiling water, and then knocked it over. Oh well, try again.

I put my boots on, we got ready, we lolled around. Soon, we thought, we will leave and we will scamper down to Camp 1, where there is a tent, and more fuel and a real working stove. Then we rolled over and went back into a stupor.

Late in the day we finally set out, Ed first with the lone ice axe, then Stephen. Finally, I rolled off the ledge and set off in their footsteps. We soon lost our way; darkness came upon us. I bumped into Ed coming back up, ever so slowly.

'This is crazy,' Ed shouted up at me. 'I just missed falling into a huge crevasse.'

Stephen arrived and Ed continued, 'If we don't climb back up to Camp 2, we'll be sleeping out in a snowdrift.'

Oh no, I knew this was ludicrous, absurd, mad.

We could only barely stand and move down with gravity on our side. But now it was dark. We were still at over 7000 metres (22,965 feet). We had no working headlamps. It was a very long way down to our ropes and the slope was riddled with crevasses. Our trail from when we had climbed up was buried. So we turned and followed Ed, the one man with the one ice axe, straight back up to Camp 2.

There was one very steep section that went straight back up to the camp. Ed got to the middle of the ice and realised Stephen and I would need the axe. He planted it firmly, then clambered up, climbed off above it and then left it stuck in place. Stephen front pointed up, pulled up on the axe, stepped up on top and carried on up. I climbed up, wrenched it out from underneath my front points and climbed up to the camp. That one ice axe was being put to very good use between three climbers.

We collapsed at Camp 2. We were f—– and we knew it. The night was interminable; unbearable. The mind shelters those things away, thankfully.

Dawn, then heat and the sun rose, and it felt so good to thaw out. Putting my boots on and lacing them up proved a monumental challenge. Inner boots, outer boots, gaiters — just too much to think about; why did they have to be so big and complicated? It was all too much. Again, we lolled, we languished, Stephen managed to make and eat a small cup of instant potatoes. Ed and I had half a cup of tepid water.

'We need to get up, get moving, or die,' said Ed.

His fingers were deeply frostbitten, the skin already dark and broken. The reality was very real for him. Ed's words were the one thing that cut through the lolling around.

Oh, that was ugly, that 'dying part'; we hadn't planned on that. To add to our incentive, Ed said, 'Stephen, you are not going to be famous unless you get down alive.'

We all had numb toes, had them for days. Acclimatisation builds blood cells but also thickens the blood, so our circulation was impaired. We could climb high, but our blood was slow. We were eating practically nothing, so our bodies had no fuel to burn. We had pretty much run out of water, the stove was a spluttering mess and only a sip or two seemed to result from our fumblings. Our multitudinous blood cells, with no food to fuel us, coupled with massive dehydration, wasn't a good combination. Nor were we exactly thinking clearly.

When you are contemplating dying, fingers and toes just aren't your top priority.

So we finally did get up. We left the sleeping bags and the stove. It was time to go down, all the way down, without stopping. There was no other way. Our life was all to be summed up in what we did that day, and we all knew it.

Ed's words echoed around in my head all day. 'Get up, get moving, or die.' Everything had to happen now. Right now. Ed knew that as well, leading us off the ledge from Camp 2 and off into the myriad of crevasses, through the morass of snow, our trail up long gone and finding a new one more challenging than even our climb up.

Nine days after setting off from the food and comforts of Advanced Base Camp, we started on what we knew was the final push back to Base Camp. Getting up Everest paled in difficulty compared to getting down. Down we tumbled, wading through the snow, wandering in and out of crevasses, over the steep parts with a whoop and across the flat parts like children learning to walk. Ed and Stephen pulled ahead of me, it was just all so tiring, then late in the day I finally saw them reach the top of our fixed ropes.

'Go, go,' I shouted and waved, and they disappeared down the hill.

Sometime that day I came back to life. Not physically, but mentally. I'd realised I wasn't going to give up and die. I had passed that point, I just had to keep moving. And I knew once I hit the ropes it was just some 40 long rappels or so down our well-known route to the bottom. I'd just need to rappel the equivalent vertical of Yosemite's El Cap. Despite the melting ice and bad rock, the anchors were all still in place, holding us tight, as much as the ropes were already stretched tight and starting to fray.

There was a line I had passed between life and death. As long as I was there, thinking and moving, I was not dead. So if I just kept moving, death couldn't get me, couldn't sneak in on me. Every moment I was lucid I was alive, and never was I more alive than when it would have been so easy to sit down and die.

Every moment, every second was a new life.

Reaching the top of our fixed ropes was like a lifeline home. The ropes were reassuring for about five minutes, then they became hard work. The snow had buried them. In the daylight, Ed and Stephen had just unclipped and passed sections by so nothing was connected. There was no way they could pull the ropes out of the deep and heavy snow and no real reason why they should have. We just needed to get down. It was all about movement, that oh-so-hard movement.

I came to the crevasse, the crevasse that Ed and I had spent four days bridging on our ascent. The rope-bridge was stretched as tight as a rope holding Everest together could be. The crevasse had widened in our absence. We would all still be up there if the ropes had popped while we had been on the heights.

On our way climbing up the mountain, Stephen had been first to see the crevasse. He'd reached it when we thought we had done the hard climbing, having already ascended an immense buttress that connected to an even larger upper snow ridge that led 1000 metres higher to the South Col. Stephen had run out the rope on the last lead, an immense vertical dihedral, a corner of sheer ice that with our dwindling gear had to be done with two largely decorative ice screws. The climbing just wasn't getting any easier and at the top he had traversed over to a gap, a huge gap, where the snow had pulled apart. He had gone up to the lip of the crevasse and peered in.

He came back down and said, 'I found a little surprise.'

Back in Base Camp we all gathered for a rest and Stephen suggested a solution 'I think we will need to do a Tyrolean. Has anybody done one of those before?'

I had, in Outward Bound, when I was sixteen. I knew enough about the fixing of an anchor, the climbing into the hole and out the other side to fix another (hopefully) bombproof anchor, and then tensioning the ropes, just enough, not too much. I knew we did it in Outward Bound for fun. It was tricky, it took time. And that was in Colorado, at 3000 metres (9842 feet), in the forest with some very large pine trees to anchor it to.

On Everest, the crevasse was at over 6000 metres (19,685 feet). Just hauling up more anchors and ropes and food and fuel for more nights would be hard, let alone doing the actual fixing of it. Tyrolean traverses were created to get spectacular photos. I'd never even heard about anyone doing one in the Himalayas, let alone that high on Everest. I argued all those points.

'Well, I don't see another way,' said Stephen.

He was right. We were blocked, we couldn't change routes, we were too committed. So Ed, the master technician and what would turn out to be a spectacular overhanging aid climber on ice, and I went back up the ropes to Camp 1 with all the supplies. At the crevasse lip we peered in. It was over 30 metres (98 feet) deep. It wasn't a clean-cut crevasse. It had ice fins and bridges, a tumbled floor with ice blocks. It had deep, azure-blue walls at the base, with pinnacles shooting from the lip into the sky. Ed went into the depths for a look and came out with stories of virtually a tunnel through Everest, of dark blue ice and a crumbling floor that creaked and ice fell away into. It sounded unpleasant down there. I was feeling lowly from being high, we needed another day to acclimatise, so we retreated for another night camping out. The next day we were up earlier, feeling better; we knew we had to do this or we were going no higher.

'Here we go again,' said Ed. We went around and fixed an anchor and he dropped off into the abyss. I rappelled down and we were now inside Everest. We wandered through the depths, through a narrow slot and before a jumbled, crumbled stack of blocks rose up I belayed. Ed went out, was sinking a screw when the immense suspended flying trapeze-like wing of ice over his head exploded. I huddled next to the wall, ice crashing and chunks flying and snow settling. I was certain he had been crushed.

'Where's Ed?' I croaked out.

'I'm okay. I'm okay. I'm right here,' Ed yelled in my ear.

He had magically leapt out of danger and was crouched beside me. To this day I don't know how he did it. Being surprisingly alive, I figured we should at the least record our adventure.

'Go stand over there and I'll take your picture.' Ed went and posed triumphantly on the huge ice blocks he should have been buried under.

'I guess we will have to go up there,' and I pointed straight up the side of the crevasse. Ed had pointed out this option before, as absurd as it had looked. Now there wasn't any other option. Like the crevasse itself, if we wanted to do Everest, this was what we had to do.

Ed racked up every ice screw we had and climbed up one wall of the crevasse, bridged across to the other and spent the next three hours placing and removing ice screws up the overhanging wall, leapfrogging screws all the way to the lip. At the top the snow went soft and he resorted to driving snow stakes into the morass and hung precariously off those. This was not a recommended technique. It is not something anyone will ever teach you. First ascensionists have to be inventors at times. Ed disappeared over the lip and I sat ever so impatiently below until a shout rang out. I climbed up and we sunk our last two snow stakes deep in a small bowl at the lip of the crevasse.

I threw the extra rope I'd carried along with us back across the crevasse and it fell short. We had to bridge the gap with the rope, it was our only option or all the climbing was in vain. I threw the rope again with a knot for weight. It fell short. We were feeling grim. I loaded up a few carabiners on the end of the rope. Overhand, throwing high and hard, baseball from my youth, thin air on our side. The rope flew high and twisted and passed around the ice pinnacle guarding the far side and dropped down the ice cliff behind. Done. Ed and I rappelled back into the crevasse, climbed back through the depths and out and up the other side and rappelled back to Camp 1.

Our second night at Camp 1. Tiny tent, one stove, world's greatest view. Dawn, coffee, movement. Ed had put in one of the hardest leads imaginable, he was tired. We crawled out and up the free-hanging rope on the ice wall above camp, then up another 100 metres up the ice dihedral

Climbing the ice slope leading directly up from the Lho La, Tibet, on the West Ridge Direct.
Photo: Fletcher Wilson

Ascending the long West Ridge that extends over a kilometre from the lower cliffs, to Camp 4 at the end of the ridge, with the summit pyramid of Everest behind. Our trail in the snow is just visible left of the sunlit snow ridge.
Photo: Ed Webster

Jay Smith at 8050 metres, headed up for our
summit bid on the West Ridge Direct.
Photo: Robert Anderson

Pete Athans (left), Randall Grandstaff (centre) and Kevin Swigert (right) in the Weatherport tent on the Lho La, Tibet, 6100 metres (20,008 feet).

The team at Base Camp, long before carpets, heaters, movie theatres or even real chairs or a table all became commonplace. From right, Robert Anderson, Randall Grandstaff, Dr John Pelnar, Kevin Swigert, Dan Larson, journalist John Meyer, Jim McMillian, leader Dave Saas and Heidi Blum.

Ed Webster leading out of the 'Jaws of Doom' on the Kangshung Face. A three-hour overhanging aid climb at over 6500 metres (21,320 feet) to bridge the crevasse and open the gateway to the upper mountain.
Photo: Robert Anderson

Camp 1 on the Kangshung Face, the author makes breakfast before heading up to bridge the 'Jaws of Doom'.
Kanchenjunga, the world's third highest peak on the far horizon.
Photo: Ed Webster

Camp 2 under the 'Flying Wing', a one-night stop on the way up the Kangshung Face and the scene of our epic two nights without tents and on retreat.
Photo: Stephen Venables

Robert Anderson (right) and Stephen Venables at the South Col, after Stephen made the first British ascent of Everest without oxygen.
Photo: Ed Webster

The author's fingers in Lhasa, Tibet, following the ascent of the Kangshung Face. Thankfully, they eventually fully recovered.
Photo: Joe Blackburn

The Kangshung Face team at Joseph Blackburn's studio in New York City for The Explorers Club annual dinner attended by Lord John Hunt. From left, standing: Norbu Tenzing, Mads Anderson, Sandy Wylie, Joe Blackburn, Wendy Davis, Robert Anderson, Roland Puton, Miriam Zieman, Miklos Pinther, Ed Webster, Billy Squier. Seated: Paul Teare (left) and Stephen Venables.

The author on the Southeast Ridge, above the South Col with Lhotse in the background, headed for the top after finishing the Kangshung Face.
Photo: Ed Webster

that Stephen had led. Ed belayed and I tiptoed out around the corner. The carabiner, the knot, the rope were all still lying in the snow on our side. I grabbed it and clipped it reassuringly into my harness and climbed up to the lip. Having the rope still there was another tiny saved moment of momentous importance. The climb seemed to be filled with those.

I sank an ice screw below the lip, then another. Solid, ice cores coming cleanly from the tube, screwed in right to the hilt — just the anchor you want when about to do something crazy. I pulled the rope tight. We had used all the fixed ropes and were now down to a single, rather thin-looking 8 mm to finish off the Tyrolean. I looked across the gap, the single skinny rope extending 10 metres out across the airy space. I regretted the placing of just two snow stakes on the far side, but we had nothing more with us at the time. If the anchor pulled, sagged down too much and forces changed, I'd hit the bottom. Not worth thinking about. Think about our new route on Everest. Think about being first across the crevasse. Take a big breath and go.

The easiest way to do a Tyrolean is to get onto the rope, weight it gently, then swing around and hang upside down from the rope with your back to the ground. Then you slide effortlessly down into the sinking abyss and attach your ascender and pull across and into the uphill side.

The tension wasn't as tight as it could be, and the sag on the first ride dropped me well below the lip when I stepped off. On the far side, it being higher, I was even further down into the crevasse. I was upside down, bouncing on two snow stakes on the single rope with no belay or back-up. Gently, ever so gently, I front pointed up and out, then into the deep snow of the bowl on the far side. I unsheathed another ice stake and drove it deep. I'd trailed a rope behind, so now we had two in place, just a bit more reassuring.

Ed was huddled back from the lip on the far side, exhausted from his previous climb up the ice wall the day before and leading us out of the crevasse, followed by our second night high up at Camp 1. But I wanted another rope out above, to back up the anchor and to keep the route moving forward. The cloud had come in and as I climbed up and away from the crevasse the lower mountain disappeared and I was alone, on our unclimbed route, just climbing.

As tired as I was, as alone as I was, having bridged the crevasse, climbing alone above it and stringing another rope out up our route was glorious, fun, the reason I'd come to Everest. And I felt that perhaps now we really were free of the cliffs and rocks and crevasses below. Even the early pictures I'd looked at and the hours spent glassing the slope through our telescope made the upper section look much more straightforward. Now being on the uphill side of the crevasse, perhaps the route to the South Col was really open? I climbed up as fast as I could, knowing Ed would be freezing below, running it out the full 100 metres straight up the slope and sunk my last lonely snow stake.

Secure, or at least as secure as one snow stake in the loose snow could be. I retreated to the lip, tensioned the ropes and slid back across. With the upper lip higher than the lower, it was a fast and easy slide home. By the time I got down to Ed it was late, he'd been huddled in the snow for hours. But we had finally cracked the final obstacle, the gateway to the upper mountain that would allow us access to the long slopes to the South Col.

Now I was back at the edge of what Ed had very aptly named the 'Jaws of Doom'. I'd thought it a bit melodramatic at the time, but now as I stood at the lip looking down two weeks later and I was headed down, I realised how appropriate it really was. I was once again faced with a final lonely slide across the crevasse. The ropes were tight, the crevasse was obviously slowly widening, ropes ready to pop.

I slid across like a trapeze artist, dangling upside down and admiring the pure blue sky. Even completely wrecked, it was an amazingly fun experience that crevasse. First up and last down, a good full circle on the gateway to the top of Everest, the 'Jaws of Doom', open and waiting for me.

The dark started to settle as I continued my descent and I was struggling. A few feet, a rest, not making much headway, mind lost and not concentrating. The thought of hot lemon drinks, of liquids floating through my now crackling dry brain cells. I was eating snow, had been all day, it was all that was left. There was some water in it, just not enough.

After the crevasse there was a long tricky sideways slanting traverse, then a 100-metre rappel down the vertical ice dihedral that never relented. That's what this climb had been like, rope length after rope length, just sneaking through, no matter how hard, no matter how crazy.

At the bottom of the rappel I had to admit it was really, finally dark, ever so dark. The headlamp was in the pack but had given up long before.

I had to dig into the snow for the anchor and couldn't find it or the next rope. It was a big slippery slope leading down to an overhanging wall, the Webster Wall, which Ed had led on the way up. It overhung at the top, where the rope hung free and it was a 30-metre drop straight down until the snow slope moderated again. I knew the top edge hung out over the cliff. I knew I couldn't afford to go down very far to search for the buried rope because I would fall off the cliff.

I knew the rope would come out eventually under the snow somewhere at the edge and lead me down. In the pitch-black there was no way of knowing where the rope went. I went almost to the edge, I cautiously traversed, I went back up to the anchor. There was nothing to do but dig for the anchor, with my skinny gloves. That didn't work, so back down to the edge I went. I had few brain cells left, but somewhere there was an iota of one that told me not to get too close to that edge, not to slip off. I went back up to the rope above and took off a crampon.

I had a plan. I would cut the rope above with my crampon, loop the rope down, then I would have something to hang from while I searched for the rope going over the edge that was buried in the snow up until it reached the edge. I was quite proud of my ability to work all this out. But crampons aren't really designed to cut static climbing ropes. They aren't really designed to cut anything, and they certainly wouldn't cut anything for me after our six weeks of climbing on the mixed ground of the Kangshung. I thought about crying a little bit but couldn't work up the energy or emotion. Here I was, stuck on Everest, my friends had left me, the rope disappeared into the snow and I was trapped in the dark. Oh well, not much to do about it, I eventually decided.

How many nights had we been on Everest now above Advance Base Camp?

Nine. Nine nights, with the last six having only dribbles of water and a bit of mixed weird indigestible food and four of the nights and days above 8000 metres, then two over 7000 metres. So while this last one could be the last straw, it really wasn't that much more. And, besides, what could I do?

I scraped a hole in the snow a few centimetres deep. I had a place I could curl up in and call home. I had no tent, no sleeping bag, no stove, no water and Ed and Stephen had disappeared below me on the mountain. I was alone with the Kangshung Face.

At some point I dozed and woke and then I started hallucinating. There was a lot of music playing, then I woke up next to a New Zealand pie cart. I couldn't get my order in. Very frustrating. Yet some of me was always present, always knowing I was on Everest, always knowing I was still alive and not dead yet. Always aware that I was still thinking, still cold, still hurting and that was good because it also meant I was alive. At times, though, it didn't really seem to matter, the living and dying part. One would just be a variation on the other. I wasn't steely willed to stay alive, I just, rather surprisingly at times, hadn't bothered to die yet.

Then morning, and warmth. I snuck down to that edge and leaned over and cast along the edge and finally saw the rope, sneaking out of a tiny hole buried a metre under the snow, dropping straight off down into the abyss.

I felt good now it was morning and realising I would never have found that rope at night and if I would have been impatient and taken one more tiny step down I would have slipped right off that cliff and killed myself. The thought of all that great climbing, and my great friends and this great route all ended in one crumpled body in a heap on the route made me feel stronger. I imagined myself there, almost saw myself crumpled in the snow. But I wasn't there. I was strong. Well, not strong, just stronger.

The rest of the day was a wasted body and mind, rappelling and rappelling, the rope clotting and icing and all those beautiful ropes all so carefully laid out already being buried by snow and becoming part of the mountain. Looking down, seeing Advanced Base Camp, far out on the glacier, seeing life below if I could just keep going, keep in the now and not let a non-moving, sitting body take over and stop the descent and this return to life.

I finally rappelled the last rope, the lead I had done at the very start of the Kangshung Face, the first day Stephen and I had started up the face. I was down.

At the bottom I had a brief feeling of regret because the route was over. The new route on Everest was complete and I would never experience that intensity and feeling of being ever so in the present again.

That initial meeting with John Hunt and putting the team together had now taken us full circle. A year later, the team got back together in New York and John flew over and we shared the stage at The Explorers Club annual dinner as I returned our expedition flag.

On his return to the UK, John penned a note on his flight home, appropriately enough I felt, from his flight on the Concorde.

Dear Robert,

Meeting the Everest '88 team yesterday was, for me, the highlight of my visit to New York and I would like you and everyone else to know that my admiration for your great achievement is now matched with feelings of personal affection for each and every one of you.

Well done, indeed!

I will treasure the extraordinary framed testimonial to my own part in the affair, to which I concur to being innocent of any of the attributes you have conferred upon me!

With every possible good wish,
John (Hunt)

I may have used up a few lives, but I'd also gained some lifelong friends, and some climbing partners, who I would share a camaraderie with for the rest of my life.

3

EVEREST NORTH FACE, THE SUPER COULOIR – LIFE IS DANGEROUS

In the evening, we climbed up 100 metres of steep snow, pounded and furrowed into hard icy rows by multiple avalanches, which really should have told us something, and reached the bergschrund. The bergschrund, formed by the glacier below, pulling away from the face above, was the line between the gentle, meandering glacial slopes and the 3 kilometres of ice crystals stacked above us all the way to the top of Everest.

There was a long reach across the bergschrund, an unbalanced climbing move where one foot was far below, the ice tools were stretched out and sunk into the hard snow above. Then the rear foot pushed from the highest level of the front points and the upper arms stretched up and everything was all out of shape and unbalanced. Then the other foot needed to be placed ever so high to clear the gap, the yawning chasm that was the glacier trying to get as far away from the North Face of Everest as possible.

Then there was the moment of trust, where it is hoped the tools are solid in the snow above, the push from the lower leg will carry one far enough to get the other crampon stuck somewhere better than the powdery, sluffing snow at the lip of the gaping chasm, get a grip, so the body can be pulled up and over and onto the mountain itself. More importantly was the mind, knowing, saying, shouting; this is it then, this is when you go from horizontal to vertical, this is where you go from being in a place you can sit down and rest to a place you better hang on good and tight with every step you take. And with every step you take you will be going just a bit higher than the last, away from safety and horizontal life below. But above is the top of the world, so off we go. We are climbers and this is what we do.

It was dark, but not pitch-black, it rarely being totally dark on Everest. Being a bit closer to the stars must help. They rode just over our shoulders.

The 'our' on this expedition was Mark Hesse, Harry Kent, Paul Teare, Jay Smith and me. We were headed up a route first pioneered by the Japanese, a single, slightly sweeping couloir that runs from the base of the North Face to the summit nearly 3000 metres (9850 feet) higher. It is perhaps the most elegant, the most simplistic and the most direct line on all of Everest. It finishes up the Hornbein Couloir, so you can add classic to the mix of superlatives. It is Everest, after all, the mountain of superlatives. In this case perhaps well deserved.

Our idea was to climb at the tail end of the monsoon, when softer snow and warmer temperatures would allow us to climb directly up the couloir and on to the top in a single push, with a bit of a nap somewhere in between. We thought 40 or maybe 50 hours would do it. So stepping across the bergschrund to spend that long on the face, carrying little more than daypacks, made that step over the bergschrund a bigger step for our brains than our boots. After the Kangshung, it was still a very worthy objective. No oxygen, small team, and hopefully very fast. That was all very appealing.

I was in Colorado and mentioned it to my father who had set up a not-for-profit corporation to run my Kangshung Face expedition. Then he'd let us use one of his apartments for Ed Webster to store and pack all our food in. He had become immersed in the Everest stories, met Edmund Hillary and was always active and hugely supportive behind the scenes. I told him I was headed back to Everest, back to Tibet.

'I think I'd like to come,' he said.

I didn't think this was a good idea. I didn't even think he would like it. As well as we got on and had travelled the world together, Tibet was rough. I'd once had a conversation with him about travel, encouraging him to go to more remote and undeveloped countries, as our trips together lent themselves to European holidays and five-star hotels in Asia.

His reply: 'Robert, I don't need to go to undeveloped countries, I grew up in one.'

Depression-era Eastern Montana had been grim — a one-room sod house, his own father who died when he was two, a dog named Touser, shooting rabbits to make a penny a pelt. My father's youth hadn't been easy and travelling now he was more apt to take the *QEII* on a cruise back from Europe with me than want to head out into the wops.

'You'll have to eat rice,' I said.

He hated rice. 'That's okay,' he said. 'I want to see Everest.'

So he came along with our trekking group, and it was fun, he ate rice and we hiked up to over 6400 metres (21,000 feet), which I reminded him was higher than anywhere in North America. So many climbers I knew had challenging home lives, had parents who either worried too much or not at all. I had none of those challenges, I had active support and encouragement, even if it wasn't on the climbs themselves. It was an area I didn't have to worry about and could go climb hard things, put myself out there and didn't have emotional baggage around my double boots. It was much easier to climb high when things down low were all happy.

Our Super Couloir climb on the North Face had some precedent, as the alpinists Erhard Loretan and Jean Troillet had completed the ascent and descent on the same route in 1986, in a rather astounding 43 hours. They climbed during the night when it was cold and the weather often better, then rested in the sun during the day. I'd met Troillet in Beijing just after his ascent, Ed Webster and I attending his Chinese Mountaineering Association celebration dinner. Loretan and Troillet had acclimatised on a host of the lower peaks in the area: Lingtren, Kumbutse and Changzheng among them, which we also put on our list, a fun lead-up to going on Everest.

Loretan and Troillet had never climbed on the North Face before their attempt, simply running out and up the Rongbuk Glacier to 6000 and a bit metres (19,680 feet) on those surrounding peaks and back to camp in the evening. When they finally got a good weather window, they were supremely fit and acclimatised. Even then Troillet had said that in the final section of the Couloir they had been moving at little more than 50 metres of vertical an hour.

'You can't let yourself get discouraged,' he told me at our dinner together in Beijing. 'You just have to keep going.'

And they had done the climb with just two people. Our original team had six, which dwindled to five, and then finally to four when Paul Teare fell ill and it was time to climb the mountain. Timing your health and acclimatisation to the monsoonal weather windows required patience and a huge dose of luck.

The Central Rongbuk also had a sense of adventure about it. Nearly everyone came in the spring and went up the East Rongbuk. Going straight up the glacier to the North Face in the tail end of the monsoon meant we were suddenly alone, just another team or two ever in residence. We were joined after a few weeks by three Italians, with a good supply of prosciutto and limoncello. They hung sausages from the rafters of their cook tent and warmed their cheese in the sun. Even the yak-herders were their friends. Our Advanced Base Camp was next to a small lake and our tents were set in an alpine meadow. It was an oasis surrounded by Himalayan peaks, with more Himalayan thar, immense bearded vultures soaring overhead and clucking snow cocks than people. We were just waiting for a snow leopard to wander through camp.

Changzheng, at 6977 metres (22,885 feet) and then Changtse, the North Peak of Everest, framed the left side of the Central Rongbuk

Glacier. We decided a quick night out high on its slopes and then a climb to the top the next day would be an ideal start to our alpine holiday.

We climbed up out of Advanced Base Camp to a snow slope on the ridge and, like a group of Boy Scouts, dug two big snow caves that looked out over the Rongbuk. Jay, Paul and I slept in one, the other housed Mark and Harry. All night I tossed and turned, memories of life in the cave with Randall on the West Ridge flashing back to me. Our sleeping bags frosted over, the stove burped fumes, dinner was crunchy noodles. In the morning Jay got up, Paul got up. I dragged myself last out of the hole, took a welcoming breath of fresh air and climbed up the 50 metres to the flat ridge above.

I stepped over the abrupt lip and onto the snow platform suspended at the end of the ridge and took two steps.

'Don't walk over there,' Jay said loudly and waved his arm to the right. I looked over and it looked fine, just an abrupt edge and then a clean drop off the other side for 1000 metres to the East Rongbuk.

I walked over to them and dropped my pack. They were all standing around silent and a bit aimless looking.

'It fell off,' said Harry. 'The cornice right there just fell off. My ice axe is gone.'

'You were out there?' I said suddenly, incredulous.

'We all were,' said Harry, 'we had all walked out there, we just wandered over, not even that close to the edge. Then we all just happened to walk back here, and the whole thing just fell off.'

I looked over at the edge again, a clean, crisp fracture, no indication of the huge cornice that had obviously overhung the face below. The team had walked out on it, walked around, even left an ice axe stuck into the snow, and wandered back. And the whole thing had fallen off. It would have been the immediate disappearance of everyone but me. I was just lucky too, though. I could have gotten up early and climbed up and been the one out there when it fell off. Now I was as stunned as the rest. We had been up on Everest for only a week and just about killed off the whole team. And we weren't anywhere near the mountain itself. It wasn't a very good start; it wasn't hardly a start at all. That was certainly a life gone right there and we weren't even on Everest.

We headed up towards the summit of Changzheng anyway. Why not? Still alive, still climbers, so climb to the top. Jay and Paul tackled the final vertical rotting snow of the Summit Ridge and reached the top. I wasn't up for facing that after the cornice had toppled off and sat in the snow feeling weak and wimpy below. I wanted to get up the mountain, but rotting, nearly vertical snow in the morning sun just didn't seem like it would be much fun. We galloped back to camp together, glad to be alive.

Above Advanced Base Camp, straight up the glacier, towering completely unobstructed and so infinitely high was Everest. It was a completely different mountain than from the south side, not only a country removed but with a completely different feel. Compared to the Kangshung Face, which really is so ungodly huge it looks impossible and, in some ways, nearly is, the North Face, while still immense, is far more appealing. Framed by the West Ridge and the Northeast Ridge, it is dominated by the black rock ridges, the cliff bands in between and the deep gash of the Hornbein Couloir on the right and the Great Couloir on the left. It is an alpinist's paradise, steep enough and with enough real features to create defined routes. But, on most aspects, it is at an angle that it can be soloed, even if you do want to bring a few friends along for fun. You sharpen your crampons, you throw in an extra ice tool as back-up or if it gets a bit steeper, and off you go.

Most climbers on the North Face are looking to go fast, to go without oxygen, and to leverage the season to suit their interests: from climbing, to skiing, to paragliding. From Messner's solo in 1980, trending right across the face from the North Col, to the steep couloirs leading up to the North Ridge on the extreme left that I would later solo, to the Great Couloir first ascended by the Australians without oxygen, to the Hornbein Couloir, the face drips with adventure and invites climbers to push their limits.

Unlike many climbs on Everest, where you start out slowly, or wander up a glacier or through an icefall, the North Face is abrupt. You are on the relative safety in the horizontal world of the glacier, then you are on the verticality of the face, where it is anything but safe. Much of the danger is not of your own doing; it is uncontrollable. Especially during the monsoon, it is simply a matter of deciding when to go, what level of risk you are going to accept, because it is never going to be anywhere near what you would call safe.

You watch the weather, you wait, then you go.

Speed and the cold of darkness are your only allies.

So up into the Super Couloir Mark, Jay, Harry and I climbed, a single line of headlamps. The first person broke trail, the rest following, swapping the lead like bike racers in a peloton. This was Mark Hesse's concept and we liked it — like a 'Tour de Everest' all in a line, drafting through the snow and straight up the mountain. We didn't have ropes on; we were all climbers and climbers on Everest don't fall. Besides, it was more fun, more committing, more 'Everest'.

Simple. Pure. Climbing.

Inside my down suit, I was soon sweating. A step, a moved ice axe, another step, repeat. Climbing third or fourth in the line up the steps was nice and solid. But, in the lead, it was slipping and punching and muttering as the snow moved and shifted and generally slid downhill. Yet being in front was being in front and all real climbers would much prefer to be in front.

Being second in line one lived in hope the step would hold, was consolidated, wouldn't punch through into the step below. With the boots buried in the snow and the crampons sucking heat out of them, my toes were perpetually cold. Varying degrees of ice cubes were attached to the front of our feet. Too hot at the core, too cold at the toes, too windy on the face, breezes rustling the skin like raw sandpaper.

Was there any joy? Should there be joy on Everest? Is it even allowed?

Perhaps in the austerity, in the commitment, in the blackness, in the air of frosted crystals there was joy, being a part of the improbable and still being mostly in control. We had started up the face as the sun set and the light and heat drained from the mountain.

Over our shoulders was the Tibetan Plateau, glowing black with distant hill shadows. When we started, we gained height rapidly, we felt good inside, we were 300 metres (1012 feet) higher in just over an hour. We didn't really get tired. We just got slower, and slower and slower.

Somewhere in the depths of darkness before dawn, I headed out to the left side of the couloir, looking for harder snow. Knee deep was liveable, climbable. Once it was up to our thighs it was just too much, swimming and pushing and slipping down as much as going up. Our drafting approach, one climber behind the other, just wasn't working as well as we would like in the sugar snow. Each of us had our own idea on route. None of it was fast so we wandered about as the climb steepened, looking for anything hard to sink our points into and keep moving.

The side of the couloir was a lot steeper, with the snow hiding miniature cliffs, steps of black rock that the front points clanked into and dully skidded off. The clank hurt the toes and bounced all the way up to the headache. And the steepness was like fall off and tumble to the bottom steepness. It wasn't plummet steepness, it was roll and tumble and cartwheel steepness. I liked the rock, though; it was concrete and solid, and I could actually get moving.

Any fall would have gone on for a very long time, though, and it wouldn't kill you quickly. It would just start to break things and twist you all up and there would be a lot of pain and then you would roll out onto the glacier and lie there all alone and very lonely and then in a little while you would die. I had a friend who did that and I didn't want to do it. So when my toes clunked, I moved very slowly. To the left, to the right, finding passage.

There is always a way up Everest; it is about unlocking the secrets. There were short moments of joy in the frosty movement up over the cliffs, of a crampon on rock close under the snow, of moving up without resistance, of taking a second step quickly and feeling the progress.

On our varying paths, Jay Smith headed straight up the centre of the couloir, Harry wove off to my right, Mark climbed up between us below. We were unroped but still climbing together; we had a sense of each other. There was also joy in that, in climbing with others who were good enough that there wasn't hesitation, there wasn't concern about abilities. I'd first climbed with Jay on the West Ridge Direct five years previously. Jay had a level of quiet competence and ability that made him a joy to climb with. He had done a host of hard new climbs that had made me very keen to get him to join our Kangshung Face team. He wasn't sure he even liked Everest, but in our warm-up to the North Face he had kept us all busy, leading us up all the smaller peaks lining the Rongbuk Glacier. I was sure he had had as much fun on those as this blast up onto Everest itself. It was so comfortable climbing with this group, just climbing without worries or concerns. Each of us was looking after ourselves and very capable of climbing through cliff bands at 3 a.m. at 7000 metres (22,960 feet) and not getting in trouble. At least not yet, not to start with.

Dawn took forever.

Maybe it was 4 a.m., maybe 4.03, maybe 4.05, because time was measured by sensation and movement and pain and thoughts in the brain, and all that was happening at a rate and pouring into the body so fast that in a minute the breath is coming and going and fogging the air, the wind is coming in around the ears with a whistle, the toes are numb, only how numb? A bit numb, not too numb, not get frostbite and freeze off numb.

Thoughts of warm sleeping bags and tents far below snuck in. Moving the arms up and pushing down on the axes provided just a bit of relief to all the twisting and pushing and turning of the leg muscles. Meanwhile, the stomach was empty, and a warm drink would be nice but only slushy water was at hand and that was inside the suit sloshing coldly against the chest in the water bottle. It should have stayed warmer, but it didn't.

All that thinking meant about a minute had passed and another few steps had been taken and we were a foot closer to the top of Everest. Which is why now it was only 4.06 a.m. It began to seem as if dawn may never arrive, and the sun had just plain forgotten to wake up today.

We crept foot by foot up and out of the couloir as it broke into the upper slopes, our trail a thin line in the snow stretching out behind us, disappearing into the depths of the expansive gully below. The sun, having been forgotten, having been given up on, finally coloured the horizon purple, a deep, only in Tibet purple. It had a glow as deep as a Tibetan monastery, a glow of the earth coming up out of the plateau. The sun was only hints of light for a long time, though; its heat was imagined, but it fired a mental spark, a match inside the brain.

The wind went funny, the breeze from the west got excited in the dawn, it swirled and played in different directions now, rushing up the face before turning and dancing down. It circled and spun and was extra cold in its excitement. It could all be imagined but it happens in the Everest dawn, again and again, until dreams of breezes playing together become real on the mountain.

Finally, the slope started to slowly roll back; it was no longer slide off and tumble to the bottom steep. It was big hill-like, but the distance stretched like a sand dune, the snow deepened, it rolled through dips and piled into hidden drifts. There were no rocks to clunk into, only wavering cliff bands that were slightly above us, or maybe way above us, or maybe forever, so long did it take to cross them.

Then the sun came up like a great circus of light and the colours spun off over the horizon and the snow turned yellow and a hint of heat was detected, a thin wave of warmth in an ocean of cold. The dawn was glorious, and we were climbing Everest and the dark cold depths of the night washed away and drips of euphoria melted in. We were alone in our climbing worlds now, dots distributed across the face.

A sip of slush, the clock rushing forward now, 8 — 9 — 10 a.m. Now the day was here it started to run away with itself. We moved right, through some cliffs, left, over some more snowy rock steps. The climbing was actually fun, thinking was fun, having to put the points on a ledge and stand up. Now we probably wouldn't go far if we fell, just tumble into the deep snow below. Maybe. So used to going up that now it is part of what we expect.

'How's this?' asks Jay.

It is a less steep spot above a few cliff bands. It looks less steep from below anyway, but when I get there, it isn't anywhere near flat, just a 30-degree slope instead of a 40-degree slope. Above it is steeper. And the snow runs quickly up into the base of the Hornbein Couloir. At least with the cliffs, we can sandwich ourselves between them.

It is good to feel like we are somewhere in the midst of so much sameness and snow and steepness rolling off below us. When the Australians climbed this section of the North Face, they aptly called it White Limbo, though they were off to the left about a kilometre. A kilometre? Probably, this face is so big it defies logic. We have climbed up over a kilometre and a half vertically, almost the same again to go. The face is a few kilometres wide. We are right in the middle of Everest it seems.

Jay is chopping and scooping and stomping out a ledge. It isn't a quick process. Down a few metres and over two is another slight indentation.

'Here we are,' says Harry. 'Start digging.'

The outer layer of snow brushes off, then a few kicks get me a few centimetres deeper. Then it is hard-packed snow, like cement, and a chip here and there is all that happens. Looks like we won't have much of a home here. It is very calm, though, the wind dies, the hanging stove is anchored and melts some snow into tepid water which a tea bag turns brown and that is lunch.

We've had 1524 metres (5000 feet) of elevation gain, no sleep, a very small icy picnic bench — none of it conducive to eating much. Harry is at home, though. I suspect he may actually be having fun, which makes me feel a bit the same. It is fun tempered by the immensity around us, the sense we have put ourselves in a position where success is hugely committing and escape is very hard.

Once the bergschrund was crossed, every step was harder, taking us higher and putting us further from where any practical human would be. Simultaneously we were headed for the top of the world, the Holy Grail.

On the tiny ledge, we put our pads under us, add soup to our tea as a second course and sit with our legs dangling over the face.

The view, the view is of the rest of the world. And today, right now, it is singularly beautiful. Tibet is deep brown and purple with orange on the fringes and deep pinks on the ridges fading to darkest purple in the valleys. There is no sign of humanity, it is the earth and only the earth, and we sit on the edge of it, cooling our heels, and move on to some mashed potatoes. We are having fun, heaven forbid. Harry lives in Colorado and we share a love of steep rocks and ice, with pine forests below. We are as comfortable on a mountain as any two people can be. We are having a picnic and admiring the view. We could as easily be hanging off the sides of The Diamond, a 350-metre (1148-foot) vertical granite wall in Colorado, as sitting on the side of Everest. Mountains, we just love them all. Harry is the ideal partner and Everest will be our only climb together in both of our lifetimes of climbing. Still, it is rather a memorable one.

Jay is still digging, much more diligently than Harry and me. He will have a real ledge soon. Mark arrives two hours later, the last 300 metres (984 feet) a murderous slogging journey for him up to our picnic spot. He is moving slowly, saying little, but says he is okay. None of the rest of us are exactly a picture of lucidity, though, so we don't really worry, not yet.

Everest tired is a different kind of tired, moving like a snail and not speaking full sentences is normal. We have burned up over 1500 metres (4920 feet) in ten hours and tonight we will climb an infinite number more to reach the summit, then come down and go home, having climbed Everest for our summer vacation.

We are climbers and knights and heroes, and nothing will stop us.

That is just how stupid altitude makes you.

Either you are one step out of the grave, or stepping into heaven, and there is no in-between.

Cumulus clouds begin to build rapidly far out on the plateau, massing up and floating towards us, but still a long way out, habituating a world that is not yet part of our concern. There isn't much we can do about this. We need 24 more hours and we will be up and down and free.

We have waited nearly two months for what we feel should be the right weather, now we are over halfway up Everest. We need to rest, drink, and when darkness settles, head for the top. The night-climbing theory is it is cold at night, so climb at night and keep warm. And when it is warm, bask in the sun and rest. So we bask.

We while away the afternoon, and drink more tea, and dig a few more centimetres into the ice and call it a bed. Then we melt more snow and have some potatoes and cheese and pretend to lie down and pretend to sleep.

The light slides off the earth. Above Harry and me, Jay and Mark settle into their sleeping bags. They rustle, they talk, they roll over, they try again. Harry and I have a final cup of tea and do the same.

A tent would not only protect us from the wind, it would also form an important emotional barrier to the great outdoors. But tents are heavy, tents mean we would have to camp, tents are for slowpokes. The list of things we don't have on this Everest climb is longer than what we do have, a real rarity. Consequently, we are experiencing the great outdoors in all its grandeur. We are having a wilderness experience in a very high place. It being the monsoon, we could well be the highest four people on earth right now. Or we just may be completely crazy.

On a big climbing wall, we would be anchored into solid rock. Here there is nothing very solid to anchor to. And there is no way you want to climb inside a bivouac sack and a sleeping bag on a bed of hard ice on a boot-wide ledge occupied by two people without being anchored somehow. So we tie into a loop of short webbing and sink a snow stake and our ice axes and then try to sleep. But as one would expect, it is not something that comes easily. But eventually the body gives up and we rest and doze.

The wind picks up, sweeping across the plateau and up the face. I go from half doze to half awake.

'My toes are cold,' says Harry, 'mind if I warm them up?'

Real men warm their cold toes on other men's stomachs. I slide my down suit apart and Harry slides his toes in, still in his socks gratefully. If it is saving toes or a cold stomach for 30 minutes, the latter is much preferred. It doesn't really cool me off, Harry's toes are soon warmer, we sip some water and go back to dozing. We'll leave in an hour for the top.

But in an hour the clouds that had been hovering out on the plains get bored with just sitting there. They come rushing across, over the foothills, blow up the face and it begins to snow. Light, dancing flakes, followed quickly by more and bigger flakes. Then monstrous, snowball-size, Everest-size flakes start pouring out of the sky. Where did that come from?

The darkness turns white as the snow piles up, quicker than can be imagined, filling in behind our backs and pushing us outward on the ledge. It wasn't a big ledge to start with. Now it is shrinking rapidly into nothingness and returning the ledge to the mountain, forgetting that, with all due respect, it was to be our bed for the night.

Compounding this, we can hear from the upper ledge that Mark's body is not happy with him. His breathing isn't good, his head is hurting. Jay is looking after him, but that doesn't include a whole lot, as the only way to feel better is to go down. If we were contemplating going down before, the snow now seals our fate. There won't be a move upward in this. As much as we want to go up, we really don't need any discussion. It's pelting snow, Mark is not well. We will go down. It would be nice to have more of a say in the decisions Everest makes for us sometimes. Changes can come without notice, without warning and with no time to think. That said, the decision, in order to stay alive, is obvious and doesn't allow time.

Harry gives up on sleeping and decides the night hours are better spent on a snow cave and starts digging. I occasionally kick a lump or two of snow off the ledge to indicate I'm helping. Harry says he doesn't really care if he has help, he is just keeping warm.

I warm Harry's toes up for him again on my stomach. Maybe by now it is midnight. I'm remembering the last time, two years before on the Kangshung Face. That was a bivouac after over a week of climbing. This is one brutal night, then a day, and my reserves are just starting to be tapped. But the sense of isolation, of being a long way out, of no rope, no real climbing gear, a huge snow slope, a snowstorm. Better to be just about anywhere else in the world right now.

We've lived a lifetime of climbing in the last 24 hours and have another to live before dawn. We don't feel we can climb down in the dark in the snow: too easy to wander out over a hidden cliff and topple off. But it is still snowing, and rivulets start flowing down from above.

We are on the tallest mountain in the world, in the monsoon, on a face we have sat watching for days on end and we all know exactly what happens when it snows.

It avalanches.

Maybe not immediately, but inevitably. The North Face just doesn't hold snow well.

The only consolation is when it does avalanche, they are the most magnificent, snow-bombing kaleidoscopes of avalanches, starting high up near the top and sweeping down the couloir with such force that if one does come there is no doubt about the outcome. I've never wanted to die in an avalanche, the tumbling and the violence and the air being sucked away on the Kangshung Face two years before was bad enough.

If there is going to be an avalanche now, it will be absolutely grandiose and will catapult me straight out of this world in spectacular fashion. It isn't worth thinking about. Thinking can get in the way and thinking takes energy. We will need all our energy to save our lives. No use in thinking.

Somewhere towards dawn, Harry has managed to dig a half-decent snow cave. Just in time to stuff the sleeping bags back in the sacks, pack the stove, just too much trouble to think about brewing up anything, and roll off the ledge, ice axes held briefly skyward, a glance into the heights of the Hornbein Couloir above, now wreathed in cloud and snow and floating more ethereal than ever above us.

Then we head down. Before I go, I wait for the others to leave, as on the West Ridge Direct in 1985, when I came down from on high a day after all the others. I am in no rush to go.

The upward journey seems so incomplete without a summit and now there seems no reason to rush down. If the face avalanches, it avalanches. I look up towards the depths of the Hornbein Couloir just above us. Above it, the summit sits in the clouds somewhere, too high above and now too far away to contemplate. The snowstorm is fading as fast as it arrived, the clouds of the night are drifting off, only the occasional lonely snowflake drifts down.

I look across the face, the North Ridge framing the view out over Tibet. The Central Rongbuk curves around and almost back upon itself at the base of the face, then is squeezed up tight against the South Face of Changtse. Then the glacier curves up to an immense ice-encircled basin at the base of the North Col. Eric Shipton was here, and then a few random climbers have climbed up this way, but it is still a real hidden gem, enclosed and difficult to access. But I see a natural ski route on the glacier, looping back under Changtse, hugging its slopes, above a set of immense crevasses. And in the basin below the North Col you are 500 metres (1640 feet) above the base of the Super Couloir where we started. It would be like getting a head start on the face, a way to put a slightly higher camp in that can be skied up to. And then just a touch over 2000 metres (6561 feet) to the top.

Why am I not over there? Little do I realise that less than six months later I'll be realising that vision and be over on that part of Everest, looking back at where I am now. It is always interesting how a big idea can start with a word, a sound or a quick view of a better way to do something.

I finally drop off our tiny ledge and into the descent, the others already disappearing below me.

We are climbing straight down in a single line to minimise any shearing on the snow.

We are a second away from death in an avalanche and invincible at the same time.

We will not slip, we will not fall, we will descend to the land of the glacier and we will be safe. Or we may not.

Going down is quick, but after a night without sleep, and very little to eat, and a bit of a camping trip out at 8000 metres, sometimes my body just doesn't go the way I want it to. Feet start out going straight down into the steps. But any little catch of the crampon, any breaking of snow, and I slide sideways and have to rebalance myself. It is oh so tiring and the body starts to cry and whimper and moan and complain. Every time I look down it is a million miles to go. How can it be this far down a mountain we were only just over halfway up? 'For God's sake, it must be the tallest mountain in the world or something.'

And it is and there is nothing to do but keep going. Around us is only snow and more snow; we are so minute, calling us ants would be optimistic. We are sand flies in the white.

Below me Jay steps down through the hidden cliff bands and drops into the apex of the couloir. It is good to have Jay out in front. This is our second climb together, both on Everest, both up high. Jay radiates competence, and if he is out front it is okay. He naturally chooses the best route; he makes the right decisions. We kid him and call him 'fluffy' for all his pile of gear. He is the master of intelligent understatement. When I am packing and say, 'This weighs nothing,' he comments:

'Robert, our packs are filled up with things that weigh nothing.' Another Jay truism.

We know that if anything avalanches now, this is where it is all going to happen. We now have the big one hanging above us if the whole face goes, and we could trigger something smaller right here that is equally deadly and it will drag us to the bottom.

The only way down is to go straight down the centre as fast as we can. Jay takes a few short glissades, decides he likes it and takes off. Harry proceeds more cautiously, then takes it up as well. I slip and slide along behind them, reach Mark and go down just in front of him, back to walking. It is easy to get lured into glissades in the Himalayas, thinking your strength and reactions are the same as at a lower altitude. I'm remembering the Kangshung and what a fool I was. No cartwheeling allowed; you only get away with that once and the sensation of being wrenched apart as I tumbled down before is way too deeply embedded to have forgotten the lesson learned.

Then in a swoosh of snow and trailing a rooster tail, Mark goes past me. I can't tell if he is in control or losing it. He slows, speeds up, slows, then gains speed and disappears over a steeper section and is gone. No sound. I'm back to being alone on Everest. Descending. I do it one step at a time over and over and soon catch up to Harry.

'Did you see Mark? He went past me going 100 miles per hour. Can you see him?'

We can't see anything; the couloir that looks so straightforward from below rolls and curves up the mountain when you are inside it. Below us we can just see Jay. He shouts something and takes off down the couloir after Mark.

Harry and I carry on at our own pace, which is as fast as we can go and still keep our legs under us. If I had been thinking I'd been too conservative before not glissading, I'm now not going anywhere near putting my butt in the snow. Walking will do just fine. We go down for an hour and it doesn't look like we have gotten any closer to the bottom. A second hour approaches and now we are in the steeper lower section, the final twist that leads out to the bergschrund.

Specks on the Rongbuk Glacier come into view. One, then two. Both are moving around. It can only be Mark and Jay. Mark has slid the last 610 metres (2000 feet) of the couloir, flown over the bergschrund and is now walking around on the glacier. It defies logic.

I count again, it being high altitude. One, then two, now three specks wandering around. Three, what is three, why are there three people? Has

Mark split apart and there are two of him, plus Jay wandering around? Too high, too long. Too much snow on the brain.

It is still a long way down, Harry and I carry on, the thighs burning, down and down, the final section to the bergschrund steepening to the point I turn and face in for the sharp ice-cliff section down to the lip.

This is where the Everest soloist Roger Marshall got to on his descent, and then fell and crashed and died after climbing high on the face the day before. This is not the place to be tired; the bergschrund is an ice climb in itself.

The final lip over the bergschrund and onto the glacier is a final huge lean back and step down to plant the outer boot far out on the slope. The ice tools release from the ice of Everest's North Face and I am free. It isn't the moon, but it is a small step from the mountain and a big step for the head.

The natural sense of self-preservation, so strongly dialled up, slides away and only then is the past tension felt, with a relaxation of life flowing back in where managed fears had kept the mountain at bay and kept it from overruling the senses.

The avalanches above still threaten; anything coming down will still take us out as much as if we were on the face. But we don't really care: we are feeling we have been up, we have come down, we won't get hit now.

We are right until we are wrong, and we won't be proven wrong today.

Even the avalanche fan on Everest is huge, extending out from the bergschrund and eventually merging into the upper Rongbuk Glacier, a miniature mountain unto itself. The going down part goes on and on. And this is only the tiny bit before what we climbed. I turn and look back up the couloir, its immensity following our transit now a reality, nearly 3 kilometres of verticality stacked over our heads.

Who were we to even think we could climb this in one push? But over halfway in a day, if only it hadn't snowed, and snowed, and snowed. If only Mark had felt better. Then I realise we are right now, today, probably the luckiest four men alive. Every other time it has snowed like this the face has avalanched.

Now here we stand, looking up, wishing we had climbed a bit higher, not being thankful we got down at all. Climbers just climb and the goal of the climb is to get up. We didn't get up, so going down doesn't feel that good.

Our doctor, Bill Hammel, has skied up to meet us. The third person is explained. Mark is okay, he has broken his glasses, is shaken, but his rapid descent has warded off the worst altitude symptoms. We work out he must have glissaded/rocketed/fallen nearly 610 metres (2000 feet) down the slope. And he broke his glasses.

We snap into our skis, we ski off down the glacier, lighter than air.

The North Face sits behind us, no longer the decider in our continued existence. It avalanches the next day, rumbling, sweeping down, clearing the route.

We are already heading down from Base Camp, packing, leaving, looking over our shoulders at the reality of where we had lived so much in so brief a time.

A year of planning, nearly two months waiting, a day of climbing up, a night out, a day climbing down.

That's Everest for you.

Back at Base Camp I'm looking up at the face, at the left side of the mountain, at all that blank space and no routes. I've seen the hidden basin up around the corner, tucked up under the North Col. It is a few hundred metres higher than the base of the Super Couloir. It would give me a head start. Above it is a whole face of opportunity, for perhaps something new, something fast. I've been high on the face now already. It is not that steep; I feel comfortable up high without a rope. Before I leave Base Camp, I am already talking to the liaison officer about my permit for the following year.

I call my father from Kathmandu.

'I didn't make it,' I said.

He had been below Everest, he had seen the heights with me, he understood the allure.

'That's okay,' he said, 'we had fun,' in the simple direct way he always did.

'I guess you will be going back then.'

He knew me well. It was a statement, not a question.

4

EVEREST SOLO
— LIFE IS ALONE

In a tent, all by yourself, in the dark, you could be anywhere.

Or maybe I just wished I could feel like I was anywhere, when where I was, was back on Everest's North Face. And this time I was all alone.

Alone in the tent meant it was a small tent, a very small tent, sandwiched between two ice chunks peeled from the base of the bergschrund. The roof was so low that the ice crystals that formed on the inside from my breath soon after I entered filled my hair when I sat up.

My sleeping bag billowed over and filled up half the space, while the other side was filled with boots befitting an astronaut, overstuffed down suit, a stove that roared at a rate unbefitting its pencil-like nozzle, and a collection of thick and chewy Sherpa potato, onion and garlic pancakes, candy-bar wrappers, soup packets and fruity drink mixes.

Above the tent, an ice wall reared 20 metres (65 feet) into the air, hanging over the tent, protecting it from avalanches but also effectively shielding out any late afternoon sun rays — the only ones that reached the North Face. So the temperature was decidedly deep freezerish.

I had daylight, I had a big sky, so it was a long way from the ice cave I had endured on the West Ridge Direct with Randall. The view out the front was of as remote a corner as one could find on Everest, looking onto the 1200-metre (3937-foot) South Face of Changtse, with the glacier sweeping tight up around its base before curving back around into the basin below the North Face of Everest.

The back door opened into a deep cleft extending down into the crevasse behind me. And on each side rose svelte, shimmering ice towers, with the tent wedged, chopped, levelled and secured between. Sandwiched tightly, as if this would create a stronger bond to the earth, to reality, which at 6500 metres (21,320 feet) all seemed a bit ephemeral.

The front door had a porch, a perch, before it dropped off 200 metres (656 feet) into an expansive basin cut with house-swallowing crevasses and encapsulated by Everest's North Face, the North Col, and Changtse, Everest's North Peak. There was no one else in this expanse; it was all my playground. It was my Camp 1 and my only camp. It was the place I'd looked down on last year, as we left our ledge high on the North Face and slid back down the Super Couloir.

Soloing Everest had been in the back of my mind for a long time. I'd often soloed routes as a rock climber — an on-site solo of a good rock route being the best fun I ever had. It was so simple. You look up, you work out a route, and you go. I'd started soloing when I first began climbing. I didn't have enough climbing partners and still wanted to climb. Then I discovered the joy in the activity itself. Direct decision making. Very little gear. An absolute connection to the rock and the mountains around. There was nothing more pure.

In the mountains of Colorado, there were acres of rock to be explored, so I often went alone, to mountains with obscure names and even more obscure cliffs. With rock shoes, a chalk bag and a daypack, I'd look up and find what I liked, climb up, and keep going if it worked out, and if not, I came down. I thrived on solo, vertical adventures; it was where I was most at home. I balanced the obscure with the well-known, and many days I would finish off a hard route with a friend in Eldorado Springs, by Boulder, Colorado, by soloing routes like the Bastille Crack, Anthill Direct or the first complex and tricky pitch on Tagger. What I had started out climbing with ropes, had found challenging and exciting and sometimes taking all day, could now be done in under an hour. No harness, no rope and no protective gear made it simple and fast.

That it was dangerous was self-evident. You had to be 100 per cent focused at all times. You obviously couldn't fall. You can't think about falling off and dying, as it destroys focus. Falling off was the ultimate and immediate penalty for anything that goes wrong when you are soloing. You have to allow for vagaries in weather, in having a margin of safety to allow for anything unsuspected. Anything from a loose rock, to ice shattering to crampons not attached perfectly. There were some vivid reminders of that. At a lunch in Sydney, Australia, with Andy Henderson, a member of the Australian White Limbo team who did a new route on Everest without oxygen, Andy recounted how he had been climbing alone just below the summit when his crampon came off. In fixing it, he froze his fingers, and shaking hands before our lunch made it immediately very real. When soloing, you have to be perfect and you have to know you can be perfect. Perhaps that is also part of the joy, a rare moment of human perfection.

On big mountains the solo challenges are exponential. Altitude fuzzes the mind and decisions are hard, with options that seem right soon being wrong. The times and distances are always huge. You carry less normally and will have no reserve if you are slowed down. But there are very big positives. You move faster and that makes you safer. You waste no time waiting and can move all the time, at your own pace. And the sense of freedom, the joy of moving over steep ground, in complete control, is never better.

It was amazing to be back on Everest after such a short break. I'd spent six months giving lectures, talking with sponsors, travelling the world. And, in between, running and climbing, always climbing, to keep the fine tuning that I thought that Everest would demand. With altitude I was comfortable; yes, it could hurt, and I had to be careful. But I also knew from the Super Couloir that the face could be steep in places, with rocks just below the surface and black ice hiding in funny corners. It wasn't a place you ever rested. Once you step on the North Face of Everest, you climb.

With my route being around the corner where no one ever seemed to go, and right up against the base of the mountain, I was hidden under the North Col far above me. Certainly, this year, I was all alone. But alone didn't mean lonely. There was always something to do: to climb, to cook, to sleep, to think.

Best to avoid the thinking, though, because too much might open the mind to questions, to whys, and to what ifs.

Introspection at altitude is best dispelled quickly. Remember the desire to be here, the desire to climb to the top of the world, to be alone and ascending Everest. Because the individual minutes, and the doubts fostered by the lack of oxygen, the cold, and the pre-dawn starts, are best to not be thought about too deeply. Best to just climb.

My new route above swept elegantly and with little trouble or jumble or break over the bergschrund and up onto the steepness of the face. There was an S-bend snow bridge across the bergschrund, but it was well supported I assured myself, and I tripped lightly across, and carefully remembered just in case a late-night return was needed. Just a foot off the bridge, icy, blue, then grey, then black depths showed the entry into a Jules Vernesque journey to the centre of the world. On Everest, some danger levels just had to be acknowledged. And accepted.

Above the bergschrund the ankle-deep friendly snow turned to hard crust and then, just as the face steepened, the North Face's shadowy positioning took control of the conditions. In the pre-monsoon, it wasn't friendly hard snow, or snow over harder snow. It wasn't even white. It was grey-black hard ice. Nothing really penetrated Everest this time of year. I realised when I was there my intimate relationship with the mountain was ever increasing. I studied the snow. I touched the rock and felt it cold, hard and brittle. I learned where it cracked, how to pull on the blocks so the loose ones were still usable, the edges that were strong and the fractures that split the rock that made entire cliffs unstable.

The absence of people enriched the mountain's personality. It was me and Mt Everest. This was a good thing because that knowing was what would ultimately keep me alive.

And while not a hard climb, the slopes were long and steep enough that any slip was going to result in a long rocketing ride back down to my death. There was really no reason to sugar-coat that simple fact.

Starts at 2 a.m. were also called for, climbing in the cold and dark when the weather was most stable, getting ahead of the day. There would be no sleeping or resting or time to complain.

Once onto the ice, above Camp 1 and it was only 200 metres (656 feet) across and up, crabbing sideways, into a sweeping couloir. I called it the Anderson Couloir (which Ed Webster would kindly add to his route guide in *Alpinist* some years later) because it needed a name and if I was going to go up and work so hard and scare myself so badly every morning to open up this route, I was going to do it with a little salve for my ego. So naming the couloir in my mind was important.

And it was a good climbing route, a very good route, sweeping up in an arc, steepening and winding up to hit the North Ridge at 7500 metres (24,600 feet) with a winding, twisty, rocky mixed bit of climbing at the end. It steepened nicely at the top and, with some imagination, reminded me of climbing in Eldorado Canyon and those steep routes with air under our heels that we climbed in the last rays of the day.

If the altitude didn't help the breathing, looking straight down between the crampons at almost 1000 metres (3280 feet) of grey-black ice running back into the head of the Central Rongbuk certainly would. On another peak it would have been a substantial route in itself, with lots of vertical, ice, rock and an exposed ridge leading to the exit point on the North Ridge. On Everest it was a rather indistinct feature, dwarfed by the North Face to the right and leading to little more than a spot on the North Ridge — still a very long way from the top.

There was always a little triumph in climbing up out of the couloir and onto the North Ridge, because the view back down was now the full 360. It was like reaching a summit, as the view doubled and the sun hit in a blast from Eastern Tibet. The ice faded to wind-blasted snow, and snow so much nicer than the ice, and the crampon points all went in softly like they were supposed to.

The mornings windy breezes would hit and the dawn cold would hang just a bit longer than I'd like, warming up visually but not in temperature. But it was morning. It was climbing Everest. It was glorious and still I was all alone at this early point in the season.

My Base Camp had just three people. My Sirdar (Sherpa manager) and cook from my Kangshung Face expedition, Passang Nurbu, his Tibetan sidekick Kassang, and my partner Margaret Seddon, who would read her way through a library of books during the long hours alone in camp. Camp was a small dining tent, a Kathmandu special edition $45 bright-blue side-walled A-frame. Water was sourced from the Rongbuk Glacier below us until spring really set in with earnest and water ran everywhere.

After a week, the usual headaches had faded, appetite returned, books were opened and I'd already been up to the base of the mountain, had my tent in place and was ready to climb. And if the 4 a.m. wake-up calls were hard, the sense of even attempting to solo Everest, to getting up and striding out up the glacier on my own was always so invigorating, so blood-rushingly exhilarating that it soon flushed the moody altitude depression and sleepiness out and had me speeding up over the rocks for two hours, to put on my skis to go up below the Face, turn the corner, weave through the crevasses and out into the hidden basins below the North Col, before creeping up the last steep section to my bergschrund camp.

Climbing alone on Everest, the outside influence of teammates was non-existent. It was very simple, but every single decision was my own.

On Himalayan expeditions, with a group, the interaction with others is the dominant element. Cooking and eating together, sleeping in small tents, sharing decision making, tied together by ropes.

Climbing together overshadows the mountain itself and the mountain becomes a stage where the human drama plays out.

Soloing is a completely different experience — it is only the mountain and you; the mountain dominated my world and my thinking. It was a direct relationship with Everest with nothing to get in the way. And I had to adapt myself to what the mountain required.

In two weeks, I'd probably become more attuned to the mountain than to humans. It dictated my waking and sleeping, what I wore, how I tried to fuel myself. If I made a right decision I was rewarded; if not, it cost me time, or comfort, or energy, or, as is often the case on Everest, all three in large doses all at the same time.

I would like to add a story of fear here. Of frightening circumstances and winning over in horrendous circumstances, but there really wasn't any of that, until the end, and even that was just a story about simply getting down alive. Crevasses didn't open up and engulf me. No yetis appeared, rocks didn't plummet down the face and almost hit me. I weaved up and over and down again and it all went smoothly. It was really only the nights in Camp 1, trying to acclimatise, if that is possible, at 6500 metres (21,320 feet) that were the real challenge.

Finally, I had been up and down and up and down and it was time to go, to solo Everest. I stomped out of Base Camp at a respectable dawn-like hour, knowing from all my trips up to Camp 1 and that it would be only seven hours. Even in the several weeks I had been making the journey, the glacier had been changing, pools opening up, rocks cascading down the sides to plunk into the water as I passed, huge mud and rock slides coming down from the heights of Changtse. The rough track of footprints winding up through the rocks would appear and disappear at regular intervals. Like most mountains, the best plan was to just go up, always up, a simple strategy that eventually ensures the summit is reached.

My acclimatisation allowed me to climb with only brief pauses for crackers, for cheese, for candy and a quick sip from the tea-laden thermos. My senses were attuned to the dangers. Cracks and pops from the glacier were benign, just temperature changes in the ice that caused expansion and contraction, sounding like car doors slamming in the quiet of a late night.

Then there were the cracks, the distant muffled but loud thunks that signalled an avalanche cutting loose, followed by a growing rumble. Those were worth stopping for, worth looking high above for, whether they were coming down from the top slopes on Everest and spreading out for miles along the base, or generated by Changtse or the slopes leading up to the North Col. All were dangerous, could roll down, pick up speed and cover me up.

Himalayan avalanches can be at a scale that they are uncomprehendingly big and go uncomprehendingly far. On the Kangshung Face we had been regularly blasted at Advanced Base Camp a couple of kilometres from the bottom of the face. On our monsoon attempt on the Super Couloir, we would be just coming off the rocky glacier over a kilometre from the base and see avalanche debris stretching all the way back to the face. The power and immensity of the snow was humbling — it would be so easy to be covered up and never be seen again.

The last 100 metres up to my Camp 1 was always the hardest. The tent was there, within sight. But the slope was so icy and steep the skis wouldn't run straight up it and I had to traverse from side to side — it would have been easier to walk, but there were just too many strange spaghetti-like crevasses that it was safer with the skis on. So I'd crab along, over ice chunks from avalanches, sloping in and out of the ice troughs, picking a path that connected snow bowls with avalanche runnels with hard packed ridges, before sneaking up the final steep slope to the porch in front of the tent. I liked making sure my porch was flat and spacious to lounge on; it was my touch of civilisation in a rather harsh world.

Reaching the tiny tent was always a relief coupled with a sense of urgency and expectancy, because this is where the real climbing started. And it would start in the pre-dawn hours of the next day. At 6500 metres (21,320 feet) — coincidentally, exactly 1000 feet higher than the top of Denali, the highest peak in North America — it isn't a hang-around kind of place. It would be up, cook, eat, sleep and climb.

The tent floor, which had been levelled when the tent was first pitched, now heaved and contorted under the thin pad. During the day, the tent heated to a point where it melted the ice underneath — unless the sleep pad covered the floor. Inevitably, the pad got pushed around in the wind and the sleeping bag, though rolled up for safe keeping, was jostled about. The result was a mogul field, which by the time I was set to make the final ascent had variations of up to 10 centimetres as the ice had melted, dipped and heaved beneath the tent floor.

Attempts to chop the floor out and level it helped little, more pads kept it marginally liveable, an aspirin soothed the blood and marginally moved the headache to a different part of the brain.

Still the night was interminable, time expanding, the watch face glowing quietly with minute hands that walked around the face at a pace that made me question if it was even working. Below on the glacier, the freezing air made the ice pop as it contracted, the glue holding it all together shifted from the heat of the day, and towers rolled and collapsed. The wind would be completely silent, then gust and whip through the space between the ice blocks where the tent sat. I knew the tent was secure, wedged the way it was and tucked into the bergschrund, it wouldn't be going anywhere. But the blasts were fearsome and impossible to sleep through.

At 2.30 a.m. I'd had enough of trying to sleep, the agony of lying there exceeding the agony of sitting up, of ripping the skin on my thumb as I flipped the top of the lighter to elicit a flickering flame. The stove roared to life, then settled back to a low growl. The fuel was cold, the air minimal, all the elements for combustion at their limits. It was too early for the stove.

Even the low flame soon took the temperature up, though, an incentive to let the hands creep back out of the sleeping bag, to brew up coffee, to eat cold potato pancakes, to think about the shirt, then the fleece, then the down suit, sliding the feet out, into the extra socks and then curl into a tight ball, encumbered in down, to reach all the way down and tighten the inner boots, Velcro on the outer boots and tighten the over boots into position, the result a mammoth foot platform that then needed a screamingly cold crampon snapped onto it.

In the pack went the tiny stove and single gas cylinder, an insulated water bottle, a bivouac sack, some noodles, two potato pancakes, a chocolate bar, some tea and coffee and against my back a square foam pad. It wasn't a real pack, just an oversized, on-my-bum pack. It didn't have shoulder straps. I thought that way I could breathe easier at altitude. If one was into carrying the lightest load on Everest, this must have been it, for a two-day attempted solo blast from 6500 metres (21,320 feet) up onto the North Ridge, a bivouac as high as I could get, then on to the top. It was 2 May, the weather was good, perhaps a bit early in the season, but audacity, so far, had been my friend.

The first steps were weighted with meaning, with portent, with cold brick-hard snow the crampons bit into, the ankles adjusting, the dull cold of the axe sensed more than felt. The face started immediately and the slope curved out for 20 metres (65 feet), then over the crevasse of the bergschrund, treading lightly as the snow fell off into the hole below, into the bowels of Everest. Then it was the crab-like 200 metres (656 feet) of an upward-trending traverse, the ankles all at the same angle, then into the ice ripples, presenting the points to the ice just so, just ever so perfectly so, time and time and time again.

Headlamp flickering, over a short vertical shelf, then traversing into the base of the Anderson Couloir, a straight shot bordered on the left by a low ridge, gradually steepening and rising out of the ice to create a distinct fin of rock before it blended into the North Ridge above. Just 800 metres (2624 feet) of no resting, no ledges, no stopping, just climbing. In the dark, the sky lightened as I neared the North Ridge.

The thin rock ridge led right up to the North Ridge, slowly levelling off, sliding out into the wide expanse of snow. I was at 7500 metres (24,600 feet) moving up in the footsteps of George Mallory and Andrew Irvine, and it was so early in the year that above me there were no pitched tents, no teams, no signs of life.

Then it was 50 metres, 20 metres and 10 metres and the snow touched rock and the route led around the right side, scrabbling up over broken cliffs, along snowy terraces, across huge tilting boulders that led for another hour up to the old British Camp 5 (now Camp 2) at just over 7600 metres (24,928 feet). The violence of the winter wind was evident, aluminium poles bent like spaghetti, nylon shredded, unable to even flap it had been so decimated. Faded red, orange, yellow nylon. Frayed ropes flapped everywhere. It had the air of a climbers' graveyard.

I sat on a cold rock and broke out the tiny thermos, a scalding cup of coffee a reminder of heat and life. It bounced in my stomach, there was no oxygen left for any sort of digestive process. Drinking and eating were more a perfunctory act, a reason to sit, to rest, to view the world. That in itself was the reason for being here. I was happy. Pure and simply happy.

The North Ridge rose above over 1000 metres (3280 feet) to the top, and it was another 1500 metres (4920 feet) down to the Central Rongbuk Glacier. Directly in front of where I sat, the South Ridge of Changtse shot out of the North Col and rose up to its long Summit Ridge. And on the left and right of its summit, the mountains, then the hills, then the plains of Tibet extended off blue-purple-pink into the horizon where the clouds and the earth met. It was a never-tiring view when every step was an ever-tiring exercise. But looking right over the top of 7543-metre (24,741-foot) Changtse made me feel like I was really getting somewhere.

It was still mid-morning when I finished breakfast and left the ledge. A curving path led up and right, an almost national park-like trail curving through the scree. How incongruous, a trail gently rising, curving, leading up into the heights of Everest. The wind was ripping itself senseless overhead and the internal breath rasped in and out of my lungs, with air that still arrived so cold inside it was like swallowing icicles. Cliff bands led out and right onto the North Face, small ledges with tattered ropes. Soloing leaves one with a disdain for ropes. They only clutter the route and get in the way.

Above a terraced band, a broad snow slope led steeply up, then ended abruptly in a rock cliff and an overhang. It was 1 p.m. Early, but I really don't want to go much higher or all the way to the traditional high camp at 8200 metres (26,902 feet); it seemed higher than necessary. Being over 8000 metres (26,240 feet) seemed more than close enough to the summit for me.

I'd thought I'd arrive at 4 p.m. I was three hours early and way ahead of schedule. This solo plan was working. Maybe I should just keep going, keep climbing?

Clouds were milling, building, boiling up from the Central Rongbuk, but that was common in the afternoon. It's the big cumulus building out of Tibet and floating across that caused concern, the clouds that we had seen build up and dump all the snow on us the previous year. But that had been the monsoon, this was the spring, the good weather season. This was the time of year to really climb Everest.

Just under the cliff and atop the snow was a cosy ledge, a metre wide, three long, sheltered from above by the overhang, with hard packed snow dished out to form a place to sit. It perfectly suited a bivouac.

It was all kind of cool, a little mini-camp all created out of a minimum of equipment and a minimum of fuss. A carefully planned and well thought through place to stop and rest and be off well before dawn to the summit.

There was just the little matter of a bit of cold, a bit of wind, a distinct lack of air to breathe. But in the sun, in the down suit, inside the bivouac sack, still in the afternoon and warmed from climbing, it was pretty snug. The stove burned with a ferocity twice its size, melting snow and producing a steaming cup of tea. Bubbling noodles followed, a candy bar. Then it was 2.30 in the afternoon.

Hmm, could be a while until I can climb. I was higher on the mountain than anyone had been that year, so there were no other tents, ropes or teams playing across the hill, all was quiet. Only the mountain and I were home tonight. The sun took as long to set as it takes to rise in the morning, slowly descending in loops through the clouds.

Can't the day just be finished, so the night can start and then the climbing can start shortly after that? The sun burned off the earth from bottom to top, the valleys grew dark, the peaks shone in the refracted rays of sun cut by clouds, the rocks glowed black.

The view, oh the view, went on and on over mountains and glaciers and into valleys and rolled off into the far high hills of the Tibetan Plateau, suffused in pinks and purples that shared their intensity with blood. It was my view and my view alone. Tonight, Everest was all mine.

Then finally it was dark, I was sitting in the dark, 700 metres (2296 feet) below the top of the world. The wind died, silence. No lights on the plateau far below, just silence and darkness, the peaks lurking in the dark, miles below, lines of peaks extending out reflecting the stars, dark glaciers now invisible.

As the sun had slid around the earth, it had taken the last vestiges of warmth with it, even if it could only be seen. The temperature plummeted. Suddenly, a planned camp in only a bivouac sack at over 8000 metres very early in May seemed a little less prudent.

People had to bivouac on Everest all the time, Hornbein and Unsoeld after their first traverse. Haston and Scott at the South Summit. Stephen Venables on his return from the summit without oxygen — true they bivouacked on the way down, but why not plan it, do it on the way up and get it over with? I'd bivouacked this high myself coming down from the South Summit with Ed Webster, though we had a tent to hide in. Then we had bivouacked again on the North Face just last year in our attempt on the Super Couloir. It saved carrying tents, big pads and the mindset was completely different. A bivouac was a place to pause, a place to rest, a place to move up from. Bivouacking was simplicity and anticipated movement; you were not really stopping climbing.

And climbing Everest with little more than a waist pack and virtually no weight was fun, right? I could climb 1500 vertical metres the first day, under 1000 metres the next, be on top, and be back down. But early

May was cold, colder than even a week later would be. And much colder than our monsoon bivouac on the North Face the year before had been. It was still like winter.

The cold came, hour by hour, and then minute by minute, creeping up through my toes. I took my boots off and rubbed my toes; they were numb. They went from numb to a bit of feeling. Now my fingers were cold. The cold was creeping in faster than I could fight it off. Soon I felt it creeping into joints, anywhere the down compressed in my suit. My knees started to freeze, then my elbows.

I stood up and moved around, stomping my feet on the ledge and stretching, like a member of a misplaced aerobics class.

At 10 p.m. I was fighting for warmth, at 1 a.m. I was wondering if I would make it. Should I just pack up and head down? I still wanted to go up; it was only the night, the dark. Just hang in there.

It was moonless, the cold was brutal, a force unto itself like I had not imagined. Boots on to hold heat, then off to massage and circulate. Hands in mittens, hands massaging toes, hands on my stomach to warm up. Keeping arms and legs loosely bent to create maximum insulation at the joints. Balaclava on, woolly hat on, down hood pulled around my face so only a tunnel of steam escapes. Still the frigid air crept in and created a tunnel of ice around my mouth.

Inside me was a hint of warmth and life, outside was only dark and a steeliness, lifelessness. I felt my mind outside in the cold. Is this it? No. There are too many cold points. At 4 a.m. I think I may make it. At 5 a.m., a first hint of light.

I sit up on the tiny ledge of snow, half a metre wide, with a rock backrest. I stuff my pad back into the back of the tiny pack. Water's all frozen. Getting the stove going doesn't bear thinking about. My legs are disconnected, numb, frozen kneecaps. I need my ice axe to balance when I stand up. I don't look up, I just start down, the first 100 metres of snow steep, not a place to slip.

The minute the crampons went on the last vestiges of feeling in my feet got sucked out the bottom with the application of steel to the rubber sole. It feels like I have strapped frozen steel to my bare feet. I feel the frostbite that has started during the night take hold and begin moving up my feet. I turn and face inward, the crab position more stable, and crawl downwards. Every placement of the crampons is like trying to hammer a nail into cement. The points jitter and poke, the coordination in my legs is gone. I'm shivering, not realising when sitting how hypothermic I had become.

At the bottom of the snowfield, there are tattered ropes from previous years, and stepping around them is annoying. I continue down the rock steps, ice axe clattering. The sun slides out of its hiding place; it doesn't quite sneak around onto the face. But the light sheds some hope. And the crabbing down the hill is helping circulation.

I've been up and down and climbed so much I am a primal creature, yeti-like, alone, just hanging on and climbing down, slowly, but with every foot where it should be now. An hour later I can stand up, the legs are working, not strongly, but they feel like legs again. The toes are still cold and bloodless, I know I have frostbite. Frostbite on top of frostbite from the Kangshung Face. Great. My New Zealand plastic surgeon's joke about prophylaxis for my toes — just cutting them all off in advance — is making more sense.

I step off the final rock step and onto the North Ridge snow slope leading down to the North Col. It is like a huge ski jump, but it always looks shorter than it is, even the descent to my cut-off into the Couloir leading down to the Central Rongbuk takes too long. I can't eat, the cold has frozen me inside out, the thought of food makes me nauseous and the water is a brick in my water bottle. A second container inside my down suit is also frozen. How can that be? I leave it on a rock ledge for my return, as I drop off the ridge and down onto the face.

It is steep and the ice is much harder than the snow of the North Ridge. I must think, yet I have a headache, a leg ache, a body ache. I am whimpering a little. I stop. I know I can get down, I tell myself aloud.

I talk to myself, I sit on the last rock that provides the last real perch before I get into the ice below, because while not steep, it is brick hard and a tiny misplaced step would see me slide all the way down onto the glacier below. How many steps is it? A thousand, hundred thousand, a million? And every one must be perfect.

Lower down the ice fades to hard snow, I reach the bergschrund, the curve across reminds me as I reach the end that I will probably not die now, barring something stupid. I will try very hard not to be stupid. I've done enough of that.

Should I have waited, should I have gone up? As the day heats up, I feel inadequate, but at the same time know the night came close to taking me to the big mountain in the sky. I know how easy that is, how soloists Michel Parmentier disappeared high on the North Face and Roger Marshall fell off the bottom of it. Both left their lives up here.

I lie in the tent, in the sleeping bag. The stove is going, hot lemon burns all the way down. I want out, I throw crackers in my pack, I escape, three long hours down, swooping down between the crevasses on the skis. The retreat to the glacier is back to life, to life-giving heat, to the sun and to the comfort of real air.

I'm lying in my tent at Base Camp a few days later. My toes are a touch black but not as bad as I'd thought. My Sherpa Passang, maker of the world's greatest pancake, translates the latest news from my Tibetan camp boy who has brought fresh food up for us from the Rongbuk Monastery.

Over on the East Rongbuk, a lone Austrian, Rudi Lang, was also attempting a solo — also on a new route but left of the North Ridge.

On the same night I had bivouacked he had also been up on Everest, at a slightly lower elevation, camped in a small tent. The next day, when I had gone down, someone had seen him out of the tent, moving around, but climbing no higher. And the next day he never appeared, and no one has seen him since.

What made me know I had to come down? Maybe not having a tent was my saviour. I knew it was still far too cold, too early in the season and made my escape as soon as I could.

And soloing I'd discovered was the ultimate test of individual decision making; it was me or nothing. It was the ultimate ownership of my own life and its consequences. Had I learned my lesson?

I returned to the heights again two weeks later, back up as high as 8300 metres (27,230 feet). But by then there were people on the route, my small cache of supplies that I relied on to climb higher, to refuel, had disappeared. I shared tents, I followed ropes — none of it solo like. Camping out with Russell Brice and Harry Taylor was good fun, but it wasn't exactly solo. It was time to go home.

But I wasn't quite finished, I'd seen a better way, a variation that would go from my camp up and right into the Great Couloir. It was elegant, it made sense, it just had to be done. It was more direct than the Anderson Couloir and would be an even faster route to the top. I liked climbing fast and light at altitude; I just needed to apply the strategy.

Owning your one life gives you the right to choose a few more.

5

EVEREST NORTH RIDGE — LIFE IS PARTNERSHIP

Why? Everest three years in a row. First the North Face up the Super Couloir in a single alpine push, then my solo attempt. Now back with a big group, and one I wasn't leading, that task fulfilled by one of my Everest compatriots, from the West Ridge Direct. And we were taking oxygen, headed for the North Ridge. I was giving up leading, and oxygen-less, solo dreams for a traditional ascent with all the packaging. 'Packaging' on Everest is all important — how the plan, the style, the logistics, the choice of route, the interaction with Sherpas, the equipment, the food and, most importantly, the team, all play together.

But this expedition was also easy, in the sense that just getting to Everest is always a challenge. Everest is never easy and just signing on to an expedition to get there and climb wasn't a good plan, I was soon to learn. I could help with funding, as I still had a healthy credit with the Chinese Mountaineering Association from my previous year's solo ascent, which we could roll over to this expedition. I could provide my experience and input from my multiple expeditions and experience in Tibet, and then I could just go along and climb.

I should have known better by now: Everest is never straightforward and trying to make it easy doesn't prepare you for what will inevitably happen. We were a traditional big lumbering expedition, with an approach that may have been fashionable and worked 10 or even 20 years before. We didn't know it at the time, but we were a team squeezed between the large national teams, with their broad support and sponsorship bases, and the efficient guided commercial expeditions that were to get into full swing in the early 90s and create the mountain environment that we have today. There were and still continue to be the smaller alpine style climbs, with a few climbers, perhaps a new route and no oxygen. But these are such a minuscule number of climbers, and they often have no desire for any visibility, that they operated mostly off the radar.

Our team, I soon realised, lacked the altitude experience and the climbing mentality to function together well from anywhere much above Base Camp. A few of us were quite capable of simply going up and climbing with a bit of carrying assistance from our Sherpa team. Others couldn't seem to work out which gaiters to wear out of camp. I've never liked gaiters to start with, and having somebody on Everest ask me which ones to wear when I didn't even have a pair — what? When guiding, fine, all questions welcome. If you come along to climb Everest as part of a climbing team, best to know which gaiters to wear and how to put on your own crampons.

The expedition fell right in the middle of my Seven Summits Solo bid, so following a non-stop solo up Aconcagua's Polish Glacier, going from 4230 metres (14,000 feet) to the summit at 6958 metres (22,820 feet) in a day, and then a hike up Kilimanjaro's Western Breach, putting a little Everest in the mix just seemed to fit into the springtime activities. With my solo ascent of Denali planned in June, if all else failed, I'd be very well acclimatised.

My friend Paul Teare, who I had partnered with in 1988 on the Kangshung Face and who had been with us in 1990, was going. Paul and I had gone back on the tail end of climbing the Kangshung Face in 1988 to climb the South Face of Aconcagua together, an epic, non-stop, 3000-metre (9840-foot) climb up a vertical mass of rotting rock and ice that was close to being as dangerous as the Kangshung. Paul was as talented, humble and as fun to climb with as anyone I'd known, and having him along on the team made it all worthwhile. As ever, there were other teams in the area, most notably a strong team of Kazakhs hired to lead and fix ropes for a Japanese team on the Northeast Ridge. This route had been attempted ten years before on a Chris Bonington expedition when Peter Boardman and Joe Tasker had disappeared in an area high on the ridge called The Pinnacles.

We were talking with one of the Kazakhs' lead climbers, Valery Khrichtchatyi, a convivial and highly accomplished climber who had already ascended a new route on Everest's Southwest Face, about their current climb when he mentioned, 'We found a body, high up in The Pinnacles, just one body.' As only Boardman and Tasker had ever climbed that high on the ridge, it had to be one of them. As two of the leading stars of Himalayan alpinism, their sudden disappearance had long been a mystery.

'Did you happen to take a picture?'

'We don't have a camera,' replied Valery simply.

We loaned them a camera and six weeks later the photos arrived. Paul Teare sent them along to Bonington. It was Peter Boardman's body resting high on the ridge, with no sign of Tasker or what had really happened. Part of the mystery was solved but not really answered. Valery showed us through a telescope exactly where he had found him. Paul sent me along a photograph that lies buried deep in my files, reminding me of lives left up high, of the cold, of the remoteness, of how lonely death on Everest could be.

Six weeks into our North Ridge expedition, our team of fifteen had whittled itself down to Paul and me, perched at the North Col. In all the areas where an Everest expedition needed to gel to be successful, we had missed out. Only Mike Bearzi and Mike Duncan, fellow native

Coloradans, had the experience and mindset to climb Everest. Mike Bearzi had been up high on the mountain with us on our previous forays. But he'd been laid low by a bad stomach, something that had seemed to dog us all across Tibet and up onto the mountain.

On Everest, though, there are no excuses or reasons for the excuses. Ultimately, it is about getting into position and then climbing. We'd made some load carries and been up to sleep in what was still called Camp V at 7600 metres (24,928 feet, now known as Camp 2). But no one, Sherpas or otherwise, had been to the high camp. So our plan was to go up to the North Col at 7000 metres (22,960 feet), rest through the afternoon, head up from the col in the early evening, then on to the 7600-metre camp for a late dinner and plenty to drink. Then we would take off again at 11 p.m. for the summit, passing through the traditional high camp at over 8200 metres (26,896 feet) just before dawn and climb straight on up to the top.

It was admittedly audacious, but at the same time, we thought it was a very workable plan based on our past climbs together. And we would be cheating as far as I was concerned at the time, as we would be taking oxygen, leaving the North Col with four bottles of the new lightweight Russian oxygen, turning it on when we got tired, cold, sad or just felt like it. I imagined us trailing oxygen like a jet stream behind us. It might just be fun too, climbing with the benefit of air, under the stars. It was going to be a last-ditch, last-minute effort, with Base Camp being cleared and the team pulling back even as we started the hike out of Advanced Base Camp for the North Col. Everyone below was working out the fastest way to retreat, as there wasn't any enthusiasm or any support for us spending a day longer or delaying our departure.

The climb to the North Col, first done in the 1920s, is a lovely snow scramble, steep enough to be fun, with the occasional crevasse bridged by a rope. Paul and I wandered up the glacier, slipped into our crampons, and as multiple trips earlier made the trip up more akin to a morning

The best ski run in the world, down the Central Rongbuk Glacier, with the backdrop of Everest North Face, the Super Couloir leading into the heights of the Hornbein Couloir, rising directly over skier Mike Bearzi.
Photo: Robert Anderson

The North Face of Everest and Mads Anderson, the author's father and lifelong supporter of all his Everest and Seven Summit expeditions.
Photo: Robert Anderson

Sunset from the head of the Central Rongbuk Glacier, Tibet, with Pumori rising above the clouds in the Khumbu Valley in Nepal.
Photo: Robert Anderson

Sandwiched between bergschrund and crevasses,
the North Face solo 'Camp One and Only.' A
safe place in the midst of a lot of unsafe ground.
Photo: Robert Anderson

Arrival at the high bivouac on the first Everest solo attempt, 8100 metres, before the coldest night of my life and the fast retreat.
Photo: Robert Anderson

The icy sweep of the Anderson Couloir leading up to the North Ridge. A single climber can be seen in silhouette on the Ridge in the centre.
Photo: Robert Anderson

Following the retreat from the high bivouac and back at 'Camp One and Only' on the first Everest solo attempt.
Photo: Robert Anderson

Looking down the North Face, our ski route down taking the smooth right-hand glacier below Changtse, before breaking left and out onto the main Central Rongbuk. Pumori prominent left, Cho Oyu centre background and Gyachung Kang right.
Photo: Robert Anderson

Mike Bearzi (left) and Paul Teare arriving at our camp at the base of the North Face, the Great Couloir at the extreme left of photo rising up towards the summit.
Photo: Robert Anderson

An amiable Sir Edmund Hillary, Honorary Expedition Leader for Everest and the author on my 7 Summits Solo project. On the floor for photos at a British Airways press conference, Auckland, New Zealand.
Photo: Raynish & Partners

The North Face from Advanced Base Camp with a very strong telephoto lens. Climbers Jay Smith (in front), Harry Kent, Robert Anderson and Mark Hesse below the Hornbein Couloir, head up for their one-night bivouac.
Photo: Warren Morgan

jog, set off up the ropes as if out for a stroll. Leaving the glacier, a steep ramp led up over a few terraces, then out and around an ice buttress, before curving back left and up onto the col. The way was marked by a set of lovely, looping ski tracks, as the well-known Italian alpinist Hans Kammerlander had been sharing Advanced Base Camp with us and had plans to ski the mountain. The admittedly ragged season with storms extending right into May and high winds had put a stop to Hans's plans as well. He had carved those very nice ski tracks down off the North Col as we had all waited for the weather window that never came. Hans had befriended our outliers group of Paul, Mike and me, and as we tired of the packaged American food, Hans had fed us on aged European ham chopped in thin slices from where it hung under the roof of his tent, while regaling us with stories of his climbs with Messner.

The last move onto the North Col for Paul and me was a 3-metre step straight up onto the flat snow of the ridge, transitioning from a view to the east, to a view straight across the North Face and out into Nepal. The North Col, unlike the South Col, 1000 metres (3280 feet) higher on the opposite side of Everest, is low enough to be appreciated, to be enjoyed, to be walked around with the ghosts of Mallory and Irvine, a cigarette in one hand and a cup of tea in the other, while admiring the view. That I'd never really been able to smoke, despite a serious attempt to take it up while punching metal in a factory in Norway, was inconsequential. Imagination at altitude is a given.

We ate noodles as the afternoon waned. We chatted on the radio to the camps below. We were encouraged to hurry up; the team below wanted to go home. We filled water bottles. The warmth from the sun faded quickly as we were under an ice cornice that sheltered us from the western winds. We were bored. We loaded four bottles of oxygen each in our packs, threw in the water bottles and set out up the slope.

The route across the North Col dropped down to a long flat apex, then began its gentle and inexorable rise up for just over 300 metres (984 feet) to the rock of the North Ridge. The snow hardened until it was crisp, but after weeks of climbing, we never even traded our ski poles for axes, just slipped one foot above the other, a gentle crabbing up left, then right, then back left, switching direction as the slope led off into the cliffs on either side, then moving back up to the middle of the dragon's long sweeping tail. I passed the point I had soloed up to reach the ridge the year before, the innocuous small rock that no one else would ever notice that led down into my couloir and the North Face.

Paul and I moved independently, skipping the fixed ropes, skipping being roped together and simply moving up and climbing. Having soloed the ridge just a year before up to the High Camp, the trail was familiar. And on oxygen, in the late evening hours, the ease with which we ascended and the speed were a completely different experience from my solo attempt. I could think clearly, I could move. I was warm. I was getting hungry. Oxygen gives you life at altitude and without it you are quickly dying.

The sun flowed down into the western horizon, into the cloud over Nepal, and faded. With darkness the wind now came in ripples, rising and twisting as the warmth rushed off the Tibetan Plateau and into the darkening sky. Two climbers, a big mountain, darkness all around, starting up on to the heights of Everest. What could stop us now? As I'd learned on my first expedition, the best climbing days on Everest are the best you will have. And the worst will come close to killing you. Or maybe they will kill you. In the meantime, we headed on and up, happily, into the dark. Headlamps went on in the rocks, the ridge twisting and meandering between terraces, rock blocks, soft snow and ice. A stray fixed rope marked the way. Like most of Everest, it was a little further than it should have been, but just after 9 p.m. we bumped into the tent at the 7600-metre (24,928-foot) camp.

We piled into the icy nylon. The sides were frozen and the Sherpas had been in residence; the floor was expedition detritus, with dirty plastic bags, half-eaten candy bars, noodles strewn about, frozen hot chocolate, a sleeping pad with burn marks. Stoves were twisted-up icy metal, pushed into one cold corner; sleeping bags were rolled into their stuff sacks and frozen to the floor. Oh well, it was only a dinner stop.

The stove soon heated the ice and our breath went from frosty to steaming. I had two strong coffees laced with hot chocolate. Paul and I talked, short sentences, in between sips of coffee and breathing oxygen. We were wound up, we were ready to go, we had enough oxygen to take the summit in one clean sweep. I hadn't used oxygen since my first expedition and was finding the ability to think and eat above 7000 metres (22,960 feet) very novel. I was warm, my muscles weren't cramping, I could eat. Outside, the night winds picked up and ripped at the tent and the temperature continued to head down, penetrating the nylon. But it wasn't the deadly creeping, freezing from the inside out sensation I'd had on the previous year's solo bivouac. It was just plain cold, and we could deal with that.

By 11 p.m. we had finished dining, water bottles refilled, oxygen bottles checked, crampons back on at the tent door. We scraped and scrabbled out onto the rocks that led up on to the incongruous little trail through the soft scree. My stomach was rumbling with uncertainty. The mix of noodles, soup, chocolate and coffee after six weeks on expedition wasn't boding well. My body had been the least happy it had ever been in the Himalayas, with a hacking cough that had cracked my ribs right at the start, often coupled with an upset stomach. I'd get a few good days, then back to more of the same, stomach twisted and cramping and too many toilet visits to count. It wasn't a pretty sight and I was hoping for a respite. And hoping that a two-day dash for the top would be done so quickly I wouldn't have time for any recurring symptoms. The top was so close in time, a dash really. Paul was the perfect partner: we never had to worry about each other, knowing intuitively where each other was, how each other felt, the route to go. It was soloing with a better half.

Paul broke trail up through the snowy terraces and recounted later that he actually felt very frightened of falling off into the black hole that was the Rongbuk, with very real ghost-like spirits floating through the night. The fact he even thought about falling was a first. More the atmosphere of Everest than the difficulty, the darkness, shattered rock and terraces of snow loosely attached, shimmering in our headlamp beams, created uncertainty and doubt.

It was very akin to being on my solo, the haunting of the North Face and the many deaths bleeding through into our climbing reality. As no one had been higher this season, the route was buried in powder snow, only the occasional fixed roped poking out to show the way. The wind came in frosty gusts, penetrating around our oxygen masks. The oxygen was life giving, but when climbing the mask obscured downward vision and fogged the glasses, a hidden curse to the blessing of air.

My stomach had gone from simple rumbling to tumbling. I was forced to stop and all the health-giving fuels from the col and our dinner were gone. The stops became more frequent, but soon we were nearly to the highest camp on Everest, touching 8200 metres (26,896 feet). It was just dawn; we were well on schedule. Paul was moving well, with frequent looks back, matching his pace to mine. I still felt I could move; I just couldn't get rid of everything quick enough to empty out my stomach and keep moving. I wasn't going to turn around, though. We sat in the rocks at the high camp. The weather was good, the route was fine, we had oxygen. But my stomach was rotten and I was moving more and more snail like. It was not a heroic situation.

'We need to go down,' said Paul. He was stating the obvious, but an obvious I wasn't ready to accept. I knew he could summit, could go on, soloing up from here was well within his capabilities and wouldn't have taken him long.

Lower on the mountain we had talked about teams, about people who left other people and went up, or down, alone. Soloing was one thing, it was accepted. When Stephen, Ed and I had gone for the top from the South Col on the Kangshung Face, I'd encouraged us all to treat it like a solo. We were too far out to help each other, and we had the experience and the ability to look after ourselves. Helping each other just added to the danger. So we were essentially soloing. Yet when we turned to descend the Kangshung, we had then become a team again, working together, encouraging each other, until we were all down safely and off the face. Even when Ed and Stephen had descended in front of me and I'd had the final night alone on the

Kangshung Face, it had been a decision I'd encouraged, with a wave and a farewell.

Now, though, Paul and I were climbing together. So we went down together. The right decisions on Everest had to push emotion aside and rely on intuition and experience. Going up until you collapse or can't get down is all too easy, as too many people had proven.

We moved down through the rock cliffs, our snowy trail to follow, down in and out of the high camp and back to the North Col. As ever it was hard, muscles burned, Everest was just so incredibly big. Time took on a new dimension, stretching out. But we had the oxygen and used it all the way back, a real way to feel better, to move quicker and to recover. No wonder it gets used lower and lower on Everest, making it easier and easier to go high. Woe the day it runs out up high, though, as like a short fuse your light soon goes out.

Paul and I dived back into our sleeping bags at the North Col. Took a final blast of oxygen. Made some restful tea and burned our lips on the cups. It was so good. We called down to Base Camp. It was still the remnants of an era when anyone summiting made the team successful, so our news was not good news. And there was certainly no sense left of a team now.

'Could you bring down any extra oxygen, so we could sell it in Kathmandu?' The query came up from Base Camp. We sipped the rest of the oxygen ourselves and carried off our empty bottles. We had a team on Everest in the end, but it was only really two of us, and Mike Bearzi and Mike Duncan down below offering support. Everyone else was back in Kathmandu in their heads already.

Despite my fizzing out at 8200 metres, that expedition was a turning point. I knew I could do Everest. I was 100 per cent certain. But I really wanted to do it my way. By the end of the year, I'd completed all the other six of the Seven Summits Solo, with a fast climb up Denali and two new routes soloed on Vinson in Antarctica. Vinson, in particular, gave me confidence in soloing I hadn't had before. The remote continent, no support or chance of rescue and being not only solo but totally alone with no other person in sight, with no radio contact, meant I was truly on my own, not just on the climb but seemingly on the continent. The joy of soloing, of making a plan, of throwing a few things in the pack, setting out on the route, to climb direct to the summit, whether it be 20 hours or 30 hours or more, I knew was possible.

In Antarctica, maps were so poor that when I'd been the first person to reach the immense summit plateau on Vinson from the east, I wandered around for a few extra hours just to figure out where the top was. Eventually I got there, but it necessitated over 30 hours of climbing to get up and back to camp. On my second solo, a long striking ridge bordering the south-west face, I'd stripped my pack to nothing, wore everything I needed and climbed non-stop from 1830 metres (6000 feet) up to the 4892-metre (16,050-foot) summit in eleven hours. I'd learned that non-stop movement keeps you warm, and if you stopped or anything went wrong you froze quickly. So the line between life and death was thin. I was not cheating death; I was controlling it. And in the process, getting the best out of life.

After our Everest expedition I still wanted to go back to Everest again. I didn't even pause with my plans to organise a new climb. On the North Ridge I didn't even feel I'd used up any of my lives, though I knew my earlier forays had put me well into debt.

From the North Col I'd been able to work out the route from the high basin tucked under the west side of the North Col, up into the Great Couloir and directly up that and on to the summit. I was convinced with the ski access to the high-altitude camp, the snow slopes leading directly up into the Couloir, and the history of Messner's solo, followed by the Australians' ascent of White Limbo, that all the upper slopes were feasible.

I had no doubts I could do it; I had no doubts about how I wanted to do it. I wanted the solo, or a small team, without oxygen. I also knew that being at the base of Everest, spending long hours alone created a sense of desperation and solitude that could potentially be dangerous. I needed the sense of partnership I had with Paul, even if it was only as far as the base of the mountain. The North Face was devoid of humanity and spirits floated there. I needed a few friends to help ward them off, to make the journey, and then I could finally finish Everest.

6

EVEREST NORTH FACE, THE GREAT COULOIR — LIFE IS PERSEVERANCE

The skis went into their ski bags, in the height of summer, in Colorado. And they came off the yak and out of their ski bags in the height of the monsoon, in Tibet. The skis were orange and aptly, or at least nearly correctly, named 'Nepal'. With alpine touring bindings and thick purple skins, they went on at 5800 metres (19,024 feet), and slithered us uphill, sliding up through the soft snow, over the glacial ice, suspending us over the crevasses and leading us up to our Camp 1 at 6500 metres (21,320 feet). The quiet, the swish, the gentle clank of binding and boot, and then, looking up, the 2000 metres (6560 feet) of the North Face of Everest. Other mountains you look up, and then maybe a bit higher. The Himalayas you look up, and then up, and then a long way further and if you are lucky, you see the top sitting out up there in a world where there really should only be clouds. As a climber, you dream of being up there, of crampons biting and ice axe swinging and striding up the ridge to the top of the world. But in the meantime, there is this quiet, swishing, ice-crystal-embodied ski slope.

Mike Bearzi, Mike Duncan, Paul Teare and I had set out at dawn, weaving and gliding upward, into the realm of Everest's North Face. No one else had yet arrived that season; we owned the mountain, or as we were soon to find out, the mountain, or at the very least, the monsoon, owned us. The monsoon, while having more snow, tended to fade towards the end of summer, but it was warmer and less icy than the spring season, and not as cold and windy as the autumn season. The key was to arrive in the summer and the snow, let the snow fade away, and then before the winds really picked up, find a short window and climb fast to the summit. As we weren't fixing ropes or placing high camps, the normal month of preparation on the mountain wasn't necessary. All we were ever looking for was a few good days when the snow stopped falling, the surface hardened up and the sun came out. It wasn't too much to ask for really.

This was the same route up to the base of the North Face I'd pioneered on my solo attempt two years previously. I felt it was a gateway to the heights that no other route had. Skiing up to 6500 metres (21,320 feet) on Everest. Who would have dreamed of that? And when it snowed, which the monsoon never lacked, the ski down could be the best run in the world. True, there were some big crevasses to avoid. You didn't want to fall. We skied in mountaineering double boots with little control. We always carried big packs. All that could be overcome, though, and after a few turns, gaining speed, the rhythm and sense of floating down from the heights of Everest was sublime.

If the snow was right and you got the turns working, it was the best ski, with the best backdrop, in the world. A thousand metres (3280 feet) of vertical that we could spin out in 20 minutes if all went well. That it took us five hours or more to come up made it even more rewarding. We had been up once before and carefully placed the camp well back from Everest, with an immense crevasse between us and the face. Paul and I knew well the power of the avalanches that came from the mountain, having been together on the Super Couloir. At times, avalanches released from just under the Northeast Ridge and swept the whole face — we wanted nothing to do with that.

We were camped 200 metres below where I'd had my solo camp and the route was the one I'd previously worked out that took advantage of the glacial terrace, but instead of then veering out left up the Anderson Couloir and on to the North Ridge, it cut across to the right and joined the Great Couloir in its upper reaches where it necked down and then shot straight up for the summit. It was the upper section of White Limbo the Australians had done; it touched on the final section Messner had soloed in 1980. It was also where Marty Hoey had tragically fallen from on one of Dick Bass's early attempts on the mountain. It was laden with portent and potential. It was a natural route, taking advantage of the high glacier, then a long sweeping slope that led up into the couloir. It was elegant, simple and a naturally direct route to the top of the world.

At our camp Mike Bearzi and I had our tiny solo tents, while Paul Teare and Mike Duncan shared a two-man mountain tent. We pitched them in a crescent with just a few metres between us. And we were well back from the 10-metre-wide, acre-deep crevasse between us and the North Face. It was a sunny and warm evening, the sun curving around the West Ridge, Pumori and then Cho Oyu tipped the last of the sun off into Tibet. By that time we were deep in our sleeping bags, while all remaining traces of heat escaped the earth in a quick rush back into the heavens. At the tail end of the monsoon it was still warm for Everest, but breath crystals soon coated the tent and reminded me where we were. What are billed as solo tents really aren't big enough for even one climber in the Himalayas. The roof is close to your face, the sides squeeze you, the head and tail are right at your head and tail. In the dark they shut out all starlight and are pitch-black. We had a full moon and while outside the slopes were radiant with light, inside it was a dark hole. With the lack of oxygen, a sense of claustrophobia was never far away. The best thing to do was sleep, but exhaustion precluded that. It was more of a collapse, the balaclava wrapped around the ears, the legs wrapped up in long underwear, jostling for space with the inner boots so they wouldn't freeze. The water bottles were always in the way when turning over; they started hot and cooled quickly. Then I dozed.

I woke to the patter of snowflakes, always sounding louder on the tent. I thought I'd go back to sleep and probably did. Then I woke again with the swish as the snow built up and swept off the tent. When it cleared another wave of snow could be heard, increasing, pelting down. Monsoonal snows are the heaviest, moisture laden, frozen up high, and were dropping like little bricks on our tents. I called out, but there was only silence. I imagined everyone else sleeping soundly.

It snowed increasingly hard for two hours. Then the avalanches started. First the rush and the crash and the rumble, sliding off the steeper slopes of Changtse just across from us. But we were uphill of the main slopes on Changtse and across the glacier, those certainly couldn't reach us, could they? Then the slides became louder, and thus bigger, starting with a deep rumble and increasing until they sounded like a train. How could that much snow be so noisy? But there were no blasts on the tent, no shaking of the poles. Just incessant snow, pelting down. How much could it snow? How long would it last? Still pitch-black in the tent. In the basin, in the dark, we were effectively trapped, surrounded on three sides by mountain cliffs covered with more and more snow building up by the minute.

As much as I wanted to believe in our huge crevasse between us and Everest, in our distance from Changtse, the snow building up around my tent and the avalanches increasing in sound and length were getting more and more frightening. But what to do? I looked out of the tent at a wall of white, and my headlamp only revealed my rapidly shrinking tent. I pounded the snow back off the tent walls from the inside, beating it out so it wouldn't collapse.

The North Face of Everest rose over 2000 metres (6560 feet) directly out the back door of the tent. The 10-metre wide, 100-metre deep crevasse just behind the tent and a kilometre of flat ground should have swallowed the avalanche. But, in the end, there was nothing to stop two square kilometres of snow nearly a metre deep when it decided to fall straight down the face.

A tent is a tomb when it is buried. The frozen nylon curled around my face and the snow packed around my body, enclosing it like shrink-wrapped meat. From a half-dead sleep, I felt the snow smash into the tent, throwing me about with a terrifying violence. There was nothing to do but bash the walls out to save a breath of air, while I felt blindly for headlamp and glasses in the total darkness. Hunched crab-like, I scuttled to the far end of the tent and ripped through the top of the door. It was snowing heavily, completely silent. The white was a wall. But I wasn't buried, I could see snow falling and I was, even then, surprised I still had a life.

One of the tents was still to my right, still intact, 2 metres away. But to my left, nothing. A clear swathe marked where it had been. My sleep-filled mind stared at the place, willing the tent to appear. Paul Teare and Mike Duncan had been in there, somewhere. The other tent held Mike Bearzi, who now poked his head out. One tent had disappeared, my tent was half gone and Bearzi's was fine. Voices like whispers called through the blizzard. Mike and Paul were there, just buried, sounding like gremlins muttering from under the snow.

In my tent everything was chaos, thrown about and half buried in the folds. Outside, the occasional roar of avalanches still echoed through the dark. One avalanche didn't ensure there wouldn't be more, not with this amount of snow falling. Our camp was in a basin surrounded by mountains. The more it snowed the more of a deathtrap the camp became.

My brain was fuzzy. What to do, what to do? I couldn't decide whether to dress for the blizzard or get out immediately and dig Paul and Mike out. While I laced my boots, they could well be suffocating. Throwing on my boots, wind trousers and down jacket, I stepped out into the storm. It was snowing so hard my headlamp barely penetrated, the snowflakes reflecting the beam back into my face. The snow was thigh deep, piled high in furrows by the avalanche, alternating drifts of soft snow with hard-packed avalanche debris and ice chunks. Only a small patch of fabric poking from the surface marked Paul and Mike's tent. When the avalanche hit, they'd made a tiny space, their faces smashed together just under the roof. They needed air.

'Sit back, sit back,' I yelled into the storm.

I could see their faces outlined against the fabric in my headlamp. I didn't want to stab them. They were pretty much squashed so tightly in place that 'sit back' was a redundant request. They weren't really able to move at all.

The first stab of the ski pole tore the tent fly open. The second ripped through the inner tent. Snow poured in. Paul and Mike's eyes were big and they gulped air through the hole. Gratitude echoed from their tiny cave. Snow enveloped them to their shoulders, the tent crushed tight against them, holding them tight and immovable in place. I realised that if the avalanche had been 1 per cent bigger or gone 1 per cent further we all would have been dead. If they had been pushed down the slope, they would have been impossible to find. Too much luck to even contemplate had held us here. This was one life, but it also held four people. Did that count for four? I hoped not, as lives right now were running thin.

The swathe of the avalanche was a twisted river of ice chunks and snow that had obliterated all before it. Mike Bearzi crawled out of his tent and we dug for an hour to free the others, the snow packed hard, already freezing back in place around them. The tent was gone once they were extracted, squashed and buried. We pulled what we could from it, like pulling gear from a coffin. Camp had now shrunk to half my tent and Bearzi's tent.

We huddled, drinking lukewarm tea from a thermos. It was still snowing, still intensely white in the darkness. At 6 a.m. a very feeble grey dawn broke through the storm. At 7 a.m. a larger than usual gunshot crack signalled another avalanche release. The roar that followed sounded like a thousand freight trains. A kilometre away and above us, the ice wall of Changtse, Everest's North Peak, dropped from the sky. It was so far up and so far away it seemed improbable it would hit us.

At first it was just a noise filling the sky and echoing around. Bearzi, standing outside his tent, monitored it like a sports announcer.

'Sounds okay so far, hard to tell. It's still coming, you'd better get ready. Oh no, it is definitely gonna get us,' he said, his voice rising in alarm.

The avalanche crashed through the clouds and came into sight in a trough below camp, then headed uphill towards us, a wave of air blasting snow into a cloud 100 metres high. Fearing burial, I dived out the tent door. A chunk of ice the size of a bowling ball flew past my head like a comet and buried itself in the glacier with a thud. I dived back inside my tent. The wave of air blasted through camp and the tongue of the avalanche took out the side of Bearzi's tent, flattening it like a burst balloon. We all stood stunned. Second avalanche, all still here, all still alive. But the options weren't good. No, worse than not good. Terrible. Were there even options?

Mike Duncan clarified our thoughts with, 'I don't care what we do, but I'd like to get out of here alive.' As with Ed Webster on the Kangshung Face when he'd said, 'Get moving, get out of here, or die,' this statement of Mike's made our choices suddenly very clear.

Bearzi, Paul and I had been struggling with an overload of avalanche thinking and mountain experience. Common knowledge says that the worst avalanche danger is during and just after a storm. Normally, staying in place would make sense. And we were trapped above the gauntlet of Changtse, which ran with avalanches all the time. Our only way out of the basin was straight down the ramp set immediately below that face.

But all the rules had been broken. Camping out at over 6000 metres, non-stop snow for the past six hours dumping out of the monsoonal clouds. Now we had gotten hit from two completely different directions. And it was still snowing. If we hung around another avalanche would soon come. Better to run the gauntlet out of here. Better to be moving, to be doing something than to be sitting ducks. Escape really was the best option if we wanted to not be buried alive.

A curious half-dawn existed, snow still dropping so thick it felt heavy in the air, like a torrential downpour. We grabbed what we could from the tents, filled our packs and strapped into our skis. It felt better, snow and skis, now we could move. Sliding downhill was the only indication there was a slope. Ice chunks the size of cars were only recognisable when I smashed into them. The roaring continued and avalanches disappeared into crevasses hidden in the storm. Looking back just after I left camp, the only distinguishable features were three ghostly figures following my tracks, abominable snowmen emerging from the cloud.

We skied over and under the slope of Changtse. Just don't fall, don't slide into a crevasse, don't tip over with the pack weight. Just go down. Bearzi caught up, the light improving, the snow starting to fade, and he carved a few telemark turns, showing the way ahead. I suspected he was starting to have fun. I followed along behind and Paul took up the rear, skiing alongside Mike. The slopes of Changtse soon faded and we weaved off into the basin below the North Face. The crevasses were big here, the skiway led left, then hard right and back again, following our infrequent wands. The light broke out below, we dropped in under Everest's North Face and stopped. Above, the clouds were still thick, snow falling. Around us the light lifted, sifted up from the glacier below. We skied down through the breaking clouds, appearing on the glacier far below like angels, floating back into life with a laugh and long swooping turns.

Advanced Base Camp had Passang in the kitchen, music, lawn chairs, alpine grass, a small lake for a morning bath, blue sheep and a small flock of fat birds wandering from tent to tent pecking stones. Every night, fifteen minutes of international news via Radio Nepal told of floods and 'the worst monsoon in 100 years'. The summer climbing season was nearly over. With the storms sweeping through camp with frightening irregularity, Mike Duncan hopped on a lone jeep and headed out over the pass and back to work. His words had pushed us into the decision we needed to escape the avalanche. The weather wasn't exactly getting any better, so a retreat did make good sense at this point.

Nonetheless, Himalayan climbers are nothing if not persistent and we were soon joined by Ed Viesturs, also looking for solo opportunities on the North Face. Now we had new company and whiled away the time together around the lake and through the long evenings. Ed was sponsored by Ralph Lauren and their Polo range of gear, so he brightened up our photo shoots and was a very welcome addition to our small cadre of climbers living the light and fast dreams of Everest. I shared all I knew of the route and our history: perhaps he could break through the snowy slopes and get up onto the heights? With his multiple ascents of Everest already behind him, he was one of the few that could actually attempt a real solo in this off-season with any degree of credibility, and we shared all we knew of routes and conditions on the hill. Maybe we weren't crazy? Ed was here, certainly one of the most talented and accomplished high-altitude climbers in the world.

The weather had no pattern, though, just washes of snow and wind with never more than a day of sunshine. There was just enough sun to raise hopes, inspire us to load up our packs and do a seven-hour, 1000-metre vertical climb back up the glacier, then spend a fear-filled night in our relocated high camp, with perhaps a quick foray out on the North Face to check the slopes, then a powder ski run back down the hill, dodging new avalanche tracks and snow-snakes as the weather closed in again. Ed placed his camp alongside ours, if not even a bit further out on the glacier, our avalanche stories less than comforting in the retelling.

By 10 September I'd given up. The permit was up in five days, and our yaks were scheduled for departure. We had only to clear camp at the base of the North Face. There would be no more of the interminable waiting, the hopes when the sun came out, the depression and fears when it snowed all night and we thought we were lucky not to die. If nothing else, two months waiting in a tent would end. Not successfully, not happily. But it would end and the privations of our 5500-metre (18,040-foot) life in a tent in Tibet would at last be over.

The next day dawned clear, perfectly clear. Our 2 a.m. start for high camp had become more bearable with practice, just part of what needed to be done. We packed enough for the day, and I threw in an extra bag of dried potatoes and a bar of cheese, just in case the weather held. Frustration had settled so deep and hopes dashed so many times that climbing Everest had faded back into my dreams. Paul and Bearzi skied up with me to clear equipment from the camp; they were done. They packed and skied off down the mountain.

What hopes did I have? I wasn't really sure, but I like climbing high on Everest, I liked climbing up there alone. And maybe, just maybe, this was it? My one shred of desire allowed a last night up high, alone on the mountain. One day the 100-year monsoon had to clear out and after two months of waiting, I could only hope this would be it. If the weather held for the night, I could at least make a final attempt. The nightmares of my earlier solo, of the ghosts wandering around the camp and the privations of altitude had all been battled into their corners. My lonely dinner was staged to keep busy, keep demons and gremlins at bay, going from soup and potatoes to tea and to sleep, before the ghosts could get me.

Three in the morning, 6500 metres (21,320 feet), a million stars overhead, no snow, no clouds, one final chance to climb alone to the top of the world. The stove sputtered to life; I sputtered to life. It was a kilometre and 200 vertical metres up to the base of the North Face on my skis. There wasn't a cloud in sight or a person in sight. Soloing Everest was the loneliest job in the world. But for once the avalanches were quiet.

Trading skis for crampons, the crispness, the exact connection to the earth began, points of steel into the ice, into the mountain. The face isn't steep enough to trouble a modern climber, nor gentle enough to let you off easily if you fall. Most soloists either fail so low they never get high enough to fall off or they get so high they can't get down and so perish in the heights.

The weather remained deceptively beautiful, but the month of snow had left the face a sloppy morass. If it was one type of snow, I could have a rhythm to my climbing. But the snow varied from hip-deep sugar to calf-deep crust.

Halfway up the immense slope is a huge rock that towers 10 metres out of the snow. It is the only rock in 1000 metres (3280 feet) of climbing, the only waypoint. So the whole first half of the journey I look up at it. It is a huge black shard of rock that we had named the Tombstone after its distinctive shape. To reach it, there are lots of steps and lots of snow. A little closer, and a little closer. The Tombstone is also the only break in an interminably physically difficult climb. Not hard climbing, just long climbing, step after step after step. Not really steep, but if you slipped, if you messed up any of those thousands of footsteps, you would certainly fall all the way to the bottom. Other climbers had proved that.

After the Tombstone, I focused on the corner, the rock corner that forms the start of the Great Couloir. It has a small furrowed-out, wind-honed ledge at its base, a little less than a metre wide and two long. It is conveniently tent sized. Most important, it is sheltered from avalanches and is a haven, a home in a very large expanse of steep ground. We had been up the face a few weeks before and left a tent and it had snowed and we had gone down again. By 2 p.m. I'd reached 7600 metres (24,928 feet). The tiny tent dug in under the lip of the Great Couloir was very welcome for the night. A miniature stove, and a single canister of fuel provided warmth. The snow was airy and it took cup after cup dished into the pot from outside the door to get a litre of water hot and make dinner: chicken noodle soup from a packet and dried potatoes. I was hungry, a good sign as it also meant I was acclimatised. I was alone but not lonely; I really liked being up this high, in this amazing camp, perched on the side of Everest all alone. And the weather was perfect, sunny, almost warm. The glaciers laid themselves out and spiralled longitudinally out through the Tibetan hills and further out to the plateau. I knew Tingri was out there, and even further out the monastery at Xegar, where I had stood and imagined myself up here on Everest.

It was important to enjoy getting where I had wanted to be for so long. So I enjoyed dinner, and I ate crackers and cheese for dessert. The sun burned low across the plateau, a blazing orange orb that sunk and then the world turned pink and then purple and finally towards darkness in the valleys. Then the ridges caught the sun and then it all flared out and the world went to sleep below me. It was pure magic.

Tossing, turning, a bit of sleeping. Check the watch. Oh, 8.30 p.m. More of the same, must be midnight? Check the watch: 9.15 p.m. Eventually dozing, sleeping and then the 'oh no, time to wake up now' feeling. Which can happen any time after midnight. I lasted until 3 a.m., the warmth of the day having long gone away and the cold freezing the stove in place on the floor. It sputtered, it didn't like the altitude and the lack of oxygen. I zipped down the door and the air rushed in and both the stove and I felt better. Weak coffee, small pack of porridge, then a battle with the boots. Sitting up compressed the stomach and there was no backrest. Reaching all the way down over the down suit was painful. The boot laces were too thin, the gaiters too small to zip, the technology that would keep our feet safe and warm a decade later not yet developed. I put the crampons on sitting in the alcove to the tent. I needed to be fully armoured up to face the world. I took up my ice axe. It was the moment, the moment to set out for the top of the world.

I was very small. The Great Couloir was great. Moving up it was slow.

From below it is one of the most distinctive features on the North Face, a natural and beautiful way to climb straight up through the rock bands, all on the snow, to high on the face. The angle only gently increases as you go higher. I pulled out my second tool, a short, light ice hammer, but only to keep my pacing and keep moving in the deeper snow sections. I kept hoping for harder snow, but the snow was furrowed with avalanche troughs filled in with more snow. There was never a place to really get moving. It was just up and up, as the couloir became narrower and narrower. I could see where Messner had moved off to the right and ascended a steep face, so I knew that was a possibility. The Australians had followed a similar route, but they had also had a rope to rappel. I didn't like the look of the down-sloping rocks, the short snow gully that ran out on shelves of rock in the Yellow Band. And I had no rope to rappel if I got up and didn't like down-climbing. This wasn't easy climbing; this was steep and real climbing and it would be easy to fall off. It scared me. So I just kept going up while inside the couloir, towards the abrupt end at the Yellow Band where it cut across the couloir. I knew from a few previous expeditions that they had climbed up here and pounded pitons and fixed ropes and done those big expedition things. But somebody had to still lead it first and while it looked steeper than the Messner route, the ledges and holds looked more incut. The cliff above looked short and steep but didn't last long and the snow started again. Maybe? The thought of real climbing, of mixed climbing over the rock with my gloves on, both terrified and excited me.

I stepped off the snow onto the rock. There were tiny ledges, and they were straight in, not sloping. And there was a rope. A rope. In the immensity of this face suddenly there was a thin, frayed rope. It was so thin and threadbare it barely deserved the name. I didn't have a harness or any gear, but as much as the rope looked from another decade, it showed someone had climbed here before. It was tied directly through a piton 5 metres above and I knew if I really had to, at least I could use it to help me down. I climbed up a short vertical section, stemmed right. The angle lessened, my gloves came off to grab a thin ledge and I moved up again. I looked down between my feet and realised I would well and truly fall off and die if I didn't get this right. 'I'm a rock climber,' I reminded myself. 'Forget all this snow stuff you have done, rock is what you are at home on, rock it what you are good at. Just climb.' I didn't think about the 8300 metres (27,224 feet) of elevation, that the rock zone and the death zone were as one this high.

I kept stepping up, reached a piton, stepped right again, pushed my feet down and the snow was above and the ice axe came back out of its holster and two more shaky, why isn't the snow any good, steps, and then I could sink the pick in and pull up and get out of the Yellow Band and back onto the snow and the upper slopes of Everest were mine. I'd forgotten I was at altitude. I crouched on the snow and the relief of getting up only let my body take over from my mind and the excitement it had in the climbing. I'd forced my body too far and nausea swept over me. My stomach cramped and I threw up, retching bile into the snow. The pain became ugly and my legs cramped from crouching down and my fingers, slowly warming up from being back in my gloves, burned with pain. My arms were so devoid of oxygen that they were wooden, dangling down. My brain was sending out dull thuds and I was gasping and wheezing to get the air I needed. My triumph over the Yellow Band had disappeared, even as I realised the final challenging barrier between me and the summit was now below me. Just keep climbing.

I'd hoped the snow higher up would be harder, wind blown, the ever dreamed of 'névé', where the crampon points would go in crisply, right to the hilt, and no further. Where the sound of your feet was a slicing of all the points into a secure platform, and no more. My head was dreaming and my feet were sunk into a reality of sugar snow, disappearing into airy, light ice crystals, hitting a rock, or just stopping once the crystals compacted. I continued up the Great Couloir; now looking left the view was out onto the Northeast Ridge, the Second Step was just off to the side of me. This is where Edward Norton had climbed across into the couloir. Where Mallory and Irvine had traversed across above me. I knew I had to break out right, to get out of the upper couloir and up into the Grey Band. The climbing shouldn't be hard, more interesting, less snow.

When I moved to escape the couloir, the snow just got deeper; it had drifted in from the west and settled along the outer edge of the couloir. At times I was wading, almost swimming, uphill. My feet had been buried in the snow all day; they were numb. I needed another day, more time, a partner to break trail with me. I'd done the hardest part, was the second person to solo up through the Yellow Band on the North Face, and now, why now, did it have to start getting dark again? I had climbed for two days straight, and I hadn't really slept. I knew I couldn't do another night. My watch read exactly 8410 metres. I stood there, snow up to my thighs, Yellow Band below, Grey Band above. All the history of Everest's North Ridge was laid out on my left. The summit I could feel above me. I remembered what Jean Troillet had said when I met him in Beijing immediately after his own two-day ascent with Erhard Loretan of the Super Couloir.

'At the top we were going so slow, doing only 50 vertical metres an hour. You just have to keep going,' he said. 'No matter how slow it feels, just keep going.'

At 50 metres an hour I was eight hours off the top, and I had no partner to help me break trail. And it was 5 p.m. It was the most reluctant turnaround I would ever do, but I had to go down. I still stood there. The sun started to fall into the horizon. I was in the shade at the top of the couloir. I just had to go down.

Now all I had to do was climb quickly down, back down the North Face, in the dark, and back to my camp. I turned and started, quickly reaching the top of the Yellow Band. It was still light; I could still see. The Yellow Band disappeared below my feet, looking twice as steep and much bigger than on the way up. I edged down and out onto the rock, front points moving off the snow, back onto the rock ledges, the lack of holds at the top making it an act of tiptoeing in balance on the front points. I reached the top piton and the frayed, pale rope. It was knotted directly through the piton and dangled down over the cliff. I didn't even want to think how old it was. I wrapped the rope around my arms in a rapid rappel technique better suited to sea-level cliffs or a hop off a short boulder when you want to get down quickly. It was quick, it was easy, it was exceedingly dangerous. The rope slid out through my mittens; my crampons scraped down the rock. My arms were wrenched and legs shaking. Looking down made it all appear so much further. I stepped onto and slid the last vertical section into the snow, shivering, huddled again in a ball on the steep slope. It was a terrible thing to have to push the body this far just to stay alive. I was retching and shivering and whimpering. The first hallucinations started then; I felt them coming. Unlike being on the Kangshung Face where they crept up unannounced, my mind was familiar with them now. Then they all came sweeping in, almost welcomed, as Paul Teare and Mike Bearzi and Mike Duncan rejoined me on the slope, having materialised to climb down with me and help me out. Then there was a short woman who I never quite saw who wanted me to go left. I knew I shouldn't go left, but she was insistent. I wanted her to go away.

I had never dropped a mitten climbing, but now I did, the mitten sliding away, accelerating, disappearing into the gathering gloom. It didn't feel like me that dropped it, though, as my left and right hand were getting confused and even though I just had one mitten, it fitted onto both hands. I had a thin glove; it was enough. I stopped to warm my hands up and night settled in, the sun finally dying, the dark coming up from below, the light fading off the face. Somewhere I had a headlamp, but it was all just white and going down and I was so used to the slope, to my ice axe, that falling was out of the question. I was a climber and climbers don't fall. I'd expected to follow my steps down, but they seemed to have disappeared, already blown away or obscured in the dark. Somewhere down there should be camp, but the couloir seemed just too long, too far, too black. I'd bivouacked up high before, maybe I should just do it again. I'd be uncomfortable, but perhaps a rest would be good. I waded through more hallucinations, more climbers, more mountains, music now starting to play, not inside my head but all around. My left hand and right hand were still confused as to what the other was doing. But I didn't trip, I didn't even stumble, I just kept climbing down. Dreams of the tent, a stove, a drink, a chance to warm my cold hands and frozen toes rose up like a mirage. But I couldn't get there, I couldn't see where it was and wandered off to the right, to the edge of the couloir, where the slope had little dished-out places, less steep. I dug a hole, a tiny half cave, a half-metre wide and a metre deep. It was enough. I took off my boots and put them carefully under my head and laid back, curled around my ice axe. My toes warmed up against my calves; I knew they were too cold. I passed out often enough to call it sleep. Time goes away no matter where you are; it is just the speed of its passing which can sometimes be painful. Sometimes the only option is to be patient with time.

A bit of dozing. A bit of warming hands, a bit of warming toes. A glance at the watch, then not allowing myself to glance any more. A belief that the night was not going to end. Or that perhaps I was dying into an eternal night. But there was pain and pain kept me knowing there was life and, as always, luckily, the faintest, tiniest hint of grey in the east eventually, turning to yellow, turning to sun and a sense that life might, just might, really go on.

I put on my boots. They were extra cold now. The morning air spun around with spindrift avalanches and started filling my hole, snow sliding down from above in the morning's wakening breezes. I took up my ice axe and continued my descent. My body was now telling me it would prefer to die, barely having the energy to shiver. When it did my body was wracked with spasms. My down suit was covered with ice crystals. It was still 1000 metres (3280 feet) of vertical down the interminable slope to the camp of too many avalanches. I'd come too far right to reach my high camp and just went straight down, down, down.

It was all a bit blurry, a bit painful, but as ever a bit more air helped. I was down below the mysterious big black tombstone rock in the middle of the slope, not so far from the bottom now. And below me there was a person, a shape moving up the slope. Obviously, a hallucination. I kept going down and the shape got closer. A climber, like me, I wasn't all alone after all. We came together on the immense slope.

'Hi Robert, how are you?'

It was Ed Viesturs.

'Hi,' I guess I said. I was still trying to work out if I was hallucinating, but he did seem quite real.

'Hi,' I said again. 'I'm okay, not too bad, I'll get down,' I said hopefully.

'Did you summit?'

'No, the snow is deep, really deep up high. Worse than here.'

'I'd hoped you summited,' said Ed. 'I was coming up and thinking maybe I would meet you and help you down?' Ed was always solicitous, an incredible climber, but with a guide's feel for looking after people. In the midst of Everest, and feeling like death, it was a very welcome meeting.

'Well, the tent is up there if it is of any use,' I said, and extolled on the wonderful, one of a kind mountain campsite.

'Oh — I'm just going for a look,' Ed said. I noticed his light pack.

'I'm just out for the day. It is pretty steep up here, though. I'll probably see you back down at camp tonight,' Ed said.

And off we climbed, Ed headed up, me down, and down, and down. It was surreal. But now we both had a track to follow. I was grateful for that as I just had no power even to go down it seemed. I made it to my skis below the bergschrund and then proceeded to topple and slide down the hill to my camp, the camp of many avalanches, and collapse inside. Ed came by a few hours later. He was up for camping out for another night and then would head down, our tents just 50 metres apart.

I had food, I had water again, I had noodles and crackers and cheese. I passed out that night, waking to darkness and dreams and a headache and drank the rest of my water and went back to sleep. In the morning, the tent burned with the sun and I woke up as tired and as wrecked as I had ever been. This was the avalanche camp, where we had come a few millimetres from dying under the snow. For now, it seemed fine, the monsoon had faded; maybe it had just been a bit early.

Oh no, I was having bad thoughts already, of what to do next, what I would change to get up the mountain. I could barely walk and yet I was working out next season's plan. Did I have enough lives for this? This expedition had used up at least two, with both the avalanche and now my solo. Everest was not treating me very kindly.

Ed came over, walking with his lone Sherpa Tendi.

'Heh Robert, how are you?' I had to admit I was as tired as I had ever been.

'Want us to take anything down for you?'

I hadn't thought of that, was contemplating leaving it all and just getting myself out of there. I wrapped up my few essentials and handed them across with a 'Many thanks Ed, see you in Base Camp.' It was perhaps one of the kindest gestures ever offered between soloists on a very high mountain.

Then all I had to do was get up, and get my skis on, and ski. But I really couldn't do that very well; it was impossible to make them turn as it required muscle and I had none of that left. With Ed's boot track in, I took my skis off and dragged them bumping and clanking along behind me down to the lower slopes, where there was air, and I didn't really need to turn, just point my skis downhill, stay upright and hold on.

Paul Teare and Mike Bearzi were in camp; they had seen me high on the face, late in the day, and then the darkness. They were happy to see me, and Ed had arrived a few hours early, dropped off my gear and updated them. I needed lots of tea. I needed dal bhat. And we needed to get out of there, as our permit was well and truly up and the Chinese were making unhappy rumbling noises from Base Camp.

At least I had finally had the climb I wanted, solo, if not to the top at least a climb, which is what I had started out to do. I'd gone back up alone and for two days had climbed towards the summit. The top still awaited, but if what I was after was a good climb, a long climb, a climb alone on Everest, I'd had all that. I just didn't reach the top. And I knew we had been lucky, escaping the avalanche by literally a micrometre of snow. And returning from my solo perhaps as tired as a person could be and still get down. I was now in debt on my nine lives, two more gone on just this one expedition. I was using up lives faster than expeditions it seemed, not the best plan for a high-altitude climber.

7

EVEREST NORTH FACE, THE GREAT COULOIR – LIFE IS FRIENDSHIP

Had I finally used up my nine lives? Was I really just cheating death? Was the fact I was still attached to the earth at all just because I had been lucky?

Perhaps, as Messner had told us in Lhasa after we completed the Kangshung Face and spent days waiting for flights out together recounting our adventure, 'You were lucky.' Before admitting in a quieter voice, 'Sometimes I've been lucky too.' How long could I be lucky for, though?

After my solo to 8410 metres (that last 10 metres important I felt; that was what the watch said and when climbing Everest you need to claim every metre you can), I had taken a year off from Everest.

After being on the North side of Everest four times in four years, it kind of made sense. I certainly wasn't tired of it, of the travel, the cultures, working with sponsors and then finally going off and climbing.

There was nothing like a dull moment, unless you counted nights in the tent in Tibet waiting for good weather. But there was always a stack of books, some good conversation with some very good company in the lower camps at least.

Every expedition had been so different. The West Ridge, the Kangshung Face, the Super Couloir, my own new route, the Great Couloir. And the teams, from big to small to solo. In virtually every season. I'd climbed all over Everest and as much as the tales of near death, horrendous storms and frostbite came through, there were innumerable moments of pure joy, of ascending into the heights as the sun came up and warmed the world and created a new life in every day. I'd had so much good climbing it balanced out the slipping away of my nine lives. The simple fact was, I really liked the whole experience of going to Everest, of climbing on Everest, preferably by myself or with a small team.

The sensation of climbing towards the top of the world with a small pack, a half-litre of water and a single lightweight ice axe was incomparable. And unlike the regular routes, the climbing could be hard enough to be interesting and challenging. Stephen Venables had compared our climb to Camp 1 on the Kangshung Face to doing the Eiger in Switzerland. The crevasse Ed and I had climbed through and rigged the Tyrolean on was a mix of audacious climbing and technical wizardry, all at over 6000 metres (19,685 feet). The North Face was immense and stunningly beautiful, remote and accessible only if you were really willing to commit to the heights. The things one reads about, crowds, oxygen, garbage and bodies, were never in evidence on any of the North Face routes.

But being safe in the mountains, the high mountains and it seemed particularly the Himalayas, and specifically Everest, just wasn't possible. I was coming back year after year after year, on climbs that were notoriously dangerous. Where was the line between adventurous, perhaps courageous, and getting killed in the mountains I so loved? I was losing friends to the high mountains, and occasionally someone pointed out that the odds on Everest were not so good. If anyone looked closer at the odds for Himalayan climbers, attempting new routes, climbing without oxygen, the surprise at times is that we made it back at all. A break would be good.

There was also the practical consideration for my year off, very practical — I needed to raise some more money. Everest expeditions were expensive.

I'd funded the first expedition I'd led, the Kangshung Face, by applying what I had learned in starting and managing my own advertising agencies, first for one of the world's most successful multinational networks, Ogilvy, and then with my own company, Anderson Hughes & Partners in Auckland, New Zealand. Having just one partner, Daryl Hughes, a marketing master and epicurean of the creative idea, who was ever supportive of my sojourns, allowed me the time and resources to pursue the heights.

When we had sold Anderson, Hughes & Partners and I'd started the Seven Summits Solo, I thought I might take a year to do the summits. But with backing from a host of great companies: British Airways, Kiehl's, Olympus Cameras, the pharmaceutical companies Bayer and GSK, NBC news and Rolex Watch, I was effectively working. I was travelling the world doing lectures, selling my photos, shooting video, speaking at events, then wrote two books, published by Penguin Random House/ Clarkson Potter. I was busy seven days a week. I needed a year off to climb less and to work more, to fulfil my commitments to my sponsors. That quickly filled up the year. Meanwhile, I was also still dreaming and looking at photos of the Great Couloir.

I felt I had the perfect approach up the Central Rongbuk, to the base of the North Face, then curving up and around into the high basin, where we could launch for the top. I had been up to 8410 metres (27,590 feet) I kept reminding myself. It just shouldn't be that hard to get into position, get the right weather and reach the summit. Just one more time and I would have it. Finally.

So back to the magic land of Tibet I went.

Our jeep from the Nepal border had pulled into Xegar, in the heart of the Tibetan Plateau, late in the day. Our hotel was inside thick walls two metres high, shutting out the local Tibetans, the very country we were in. It could quickly be turned from a no-star hotel to a fortress and soldiers moved in to defend the area at a moment's notice. Rooms were stale, orange bedspreads pale with washing. The handles on the sink turned but no water came out. Next to the toilet sat a bucket to be refilled with water from a well outside to 'flush' the toilet. It was as if the design had been taken from a hotel magazine of what a hotel should look like, overlaid with some Chinese design, and then transported to a land where water, electricity and maintenance were sporadic at best.

Mike Bearzi and I were back, along with Eric Winkelman, a talented climber who had climbed with Mike and made the first free ascent of Cerro Torre from the Patagonian ice cap. Eric was also an early climbing partner of Alex Lowe's, having climbed in Yosemite and Canada, doing new routes and honing their skills together. Eric hoped that perhaps Mike's and my earlier experience on Everest made an ascent of the North Face more likely. With our lessons learned, he would come along and perhaps coast along on our knowledge to the summit. I appreciated that sense of confidence in us.

The next day in Tibet we wandered over to the base of a 500-metre-high ridge above the Xegar Monastery. It rose up in a series of castle-like walls to a pinpoint summit festooned with prayer flags. The final ridge was a fine solo, exposed, loose and dangerous, and way too high to fall off, very good practice for the rocks of Everest. From the top we looked far out to the south and could just see the plume of Everest streaming away into the blue. I felt like I was touching the heights already, and it was great to be back with such a small, talented and fun team.

The Xegar hotel was at an ideal altitude to acclimatise, set at the foot of the suitably picturesque monastery. But the putrid food, draughty rooms, dust and wind didn't lend themselves to any level of enjoyment. So the next day we jumped back in the jeep for the ride up the Pang La Pass. We'd be going from the 1400-metre (4600-foot) elevation in Kathmandu up to 5150 metres (16,900 feet) at Base Camp in four days, but with our own cook, food and tents, it was a better alternative with our small group of climbers. Our pre-dawn start didn't really wake us up until the top of the pass. From there, standing directly to the south, was Everest, looking like you would expect the tallest mountain in the world to look.

The North Face jutted straight into the air through ridges and ramparts, snowfields and ice cliffs; the top shot right up into the white plume, pulling Everest into the heavens. The Pang La Pass was over 5000 metres (17,000 feet) high, while the top of Everest, 3500 vertical metres higher, dwarfed everything around it. It was a view that, weakened by altitude, thousands of kilometres of travel and the sudden glaring reality of the peak in its early morning clarity, made me feel very feeble and small.

With memories of the avalanche burying me in the tent two years previously, and other soloists' misadventures, the history of small teams and soloists on Everest wasn't exactly inspirational. There was the ice cliff Roger Marshall fell and died from at the base of the North Face, the rock where Rudi Lang decided to stay an extra night at and then disappeared from, and the couloir where Michel Parmentier climbed up into and was never seen again.

The challenge with visiting Everest more than once was that the knowledge and experience gained was balanced with knowing how much it could hurt at times, the nights and days of cold and nausea. There was the ongoing uncertainty of unknown weather and waiting, then climbing into the far reaches of the heights, with no ropes or oxygen or Sherpas for company or to help with load carrying. There was that knowing the pure ugliness of altitude that robbed the brain of thought and desire. Then, underneath, from the distance of the Pang La, there was looking around at friends, albeit a small group, and knowing you weren't alone in dreaming, and feeling the breeze of inspiration that stirs the soul at levels nothing else does. Then the wind howled, we got back in the jeeps and rushed down the pass and on to Base Camp.

The road followed the riverbed up the wide valley, then crossed a lone cement bridge and curved around and up through broad yak pastures into the Rongbuk Valley. The valley was made famous during the British attempts on Everest in the 1920s as they hiked up past the Rongbuk Monastery and on to Everest Base Camp. The hills alongside soon grew into cliffs, while the road wove a precipitous path along the river.

White-capped peaks poked out from behind the cliffs, the air thinned yet again, a breeze blew down the glacier and at the end of a long sweeping corner, the North Face of Everest came into view, dominating the entire head of the valley. The jeep toiled up the hill, engine gasping in the thin air, crossed a wide boulder-filled stream, bounced over the round granite rocks embedded in the sandy soil and swept onto the smooth moraine at the foot of the glacier.

During the monsoon, Base Camp is often deserted, the hundreds that populate it during the pre-monsoon season long gone and only the occasional tourist jeep rolling up in late morning, a few disgruntled people heavily bundled and heavily medicated for headaches step out, have a slow and aimless wander around, line up for a photo, throw up their lunch, and then head back down the road. Luckily for us, Base Camp was little more than a way-station, where jeep power was replaced by yak power for a move 10 kilometres up the glacier, to Advanced Base Camp, our real home for the next two months and a place rarely visited by anyone. We liked it that way, the mountain our focus, life below disappearing.

We had all of six yaks, carrying 60 kilos (132 pounds) each, beasts that by now I had learned to load and unload to a standard that even the yak-herders seemed to tolerate. The herders were wild men I had grown to like and trust, born into a set of clothes they seemingly still wore, with large chunks of coral in their ears, layers of rough yak wool slung over their shoulders and drooping dark trousers held up with a twist of rainbow threads wound around their waist. With my many expeditions,

Paul Teare threading crevasses and skiing up the Central Rongbuk, West Ridge behind in cloud to the left.
Photo: Robert Anderson

Mike Bearzi (left) and Paul Teare, climbing partners from a multitude of Everest expeditions, to the South Face of Aconcagua to Shishapangma in winter. Advanced Base Camp, Central Rongbuk.
Photo: Robert Anderson

Running the gauntlet between the avalanche slopes of Changtse on the right and the huge crevasses of the Central Rongbuk Glacier on the left, Mike Bearzi threads the needle to Camp 1 below the North Face.
Photo: Robert Anderson

The cliff camp at the base of the Great Couloir, 7600 metres, and the only half-decent camp in 2000 metres of climbing. Eric Winkleman (left) and Mike Bearzi arrive for an early dinner.
Photo: Robert Anderson

Mike Bearzi heading up the Great Couloir, 7800 metres and counting, dawn shining off the summit slopes of Everest.
Photo: Robert Anderson

In the midst of an avalanche on the descent, Mike Bearzi makes a quicker than expected descent down the North Face following our four days in the heights.
Photo: Robert Anderson

The Catalan North Face team creating their classic cultural pyramid. Author being crushed bottom left, Mike Bearzi just above him, Araceli Segara going for the summit.
Photo: Passang Nurbu

The winter road across Tibet, over the high passes and on to Tingri, Tibet.
Photo: Robert Anderson

Above: Load carrying up the Central Rongbuk in winter, a superbly crisp day on the heights of Everest above.
Photo: Robert Anderson

Below: Headed for Advanced Base Camp, the trail a swathe of ice, two Sherpas and one dog on the way up the East Rongbuk.
Photo: Robert Anderson

Dr Fred Ziel, fixing Sherpa fingers at Base Camp, with Borge Ousland (right).
Photo: Robert Anderson.

Sibusiso Vilane (left) and the author on the summit of Everest.
Photo: David Hamilton

The Hillary Step in 2010. Years of successful guided ascents, climbers with the same weather reports, improved oxygen, and the lines to the top just get longer. Fortunately, we were already headed down.
Photo: Robert Anderson

some of them remembered me, inviting me for tea in the morning and for the local liquor, rakshi, in the evenings. I'd learned it made no difference what schedule we wanted to go up to the mountain, the yak-herders would go when they wanted and carry what they wanted. It was easier to just fit into their plans. Discussing the time of day with someone who has never worn a watch just didn't make much sense. Passang, our Sherpa who had now accompanied me on five Everest expeditions, came into his own, speaking fluent Tibetan learned in his youth while slepping goods back and forth over the Nepali high passes into Tibet, negotiated loads and our departure.

We wandered out of Base Camp, following the steady yak pace that in the morning seemed slow, and by the afternoon seemed much quicker, first over the flat rock-strewn gravel moraine, then into a tight confining valley with a rock-embedded mud cliff to the left and the glacier rising up to the right soon left all traces of civilisation behind. An hour above Base Camp, the East Rongbuk Stream boiled down out of the hidden gorge leading to the North Col, scene of the original British attempts on the North Ridge. Leaping from stone to stone over the turbulent stream, we crossed the gateway to the inner sanctum of Everest's North Face.

Advanced Base Camp was a patch of heaven on the edge of the glacier. It was impossible to imagine a more comfortable — or spectacular — setting. Located on a grassy terrace 100 metres (328 feet) above the Central Rongbuk Glacier, small lakes 20 metres across and 50 metres long reflected the Himalayan peaks surrounding the camp. Lush grassy tussocks framed the pools, puffs of intense green sprouting from the alpine grasses growing thick, short and luxuriantly around the water. The camp was tight against the hill, on the inside of a corner in the glacial valley, so the wind whistled around, but rarely directly through camp. It was a rare and precious oasis tucked up underneath the highest peak in the world.

Directly above Advanced Base Camp on the left side of the Central Rongbuk Glacier rose Changzheng, a stellar, if admittedly little known and little climbed, Himalayan peak. This makes it even more appealing, a hidden gem in the shadow of Everest. Changzheng, at 6977 metres (22,885 feet) is higher than Aconcagua in the Argentinian Andes, the tallest peak outside of the Himalayas, and anywhere besides the Himalayas it would be a very worthy objective. A rocky ridge led up to a knife-edged cornice with a huge plume of ice hanging out over the East Rongbuk Glacier. Its true allure was its obscurity, its dangerous climbing, its position straight up out of the valley, and its wild, out-in-the-clouds summit cornice. And being just a few kilometres from Everest, you get a sense of the big mountain right there in front of you, looking across at you on the climb.

Jay Smith and Paul Teare had climbed Changzheng in preparation for our two-day attempt on the Super Couloir, but that year I had baulked at a final vertical section of crumbling, rotting ice that barred the last 200 metres leading up to the summit. With a few thousand metres of exposure, climbing with no ropes or protection, it wasn't the place to make a mistake. The thigh-high deep snow that led up to the holey, crackly ice didn't provide a single solid crampon or tool placement. Jay and Paul had come down from the summit and their tale of weak ice and balancing out across the vertical wall barring the summit, weighting each foot only a fraction at a time so the slope didn't give way, only convinced me that my own retreat was a good personal decision. After all, Changzheng was just supposed to be a warm-up for Everest, a chance to get high and acclimatise. Actually reaching the top wasn't the real objective. Of course, then I went away and thought about it for a few years and now I was back under Changzheng's slope again. And reaching the top really was the objective this time. Why get so close and just stop? It was like reaching the South Summit of Everest; I really liked doing the final few metres and getting to the very summit of peaks I was climbing.

I was climbing with Eric. We had teamed up together and come to Everest to make what I hoped would be our final grand ascent of the route up the Great Couloir. Mike Bearzi was always slow acclimatising, so Eric Winkelman and I decided to attempt a one day climb of Changzheng prior to moving on to Everest. Eric had coaching and confidence-building skills beyond just his mastery of steep ice, and he encouraged me slowly across the final ice wall, a step at a time, balancing our weight between front points and the picks of our loosely placed ice tools. Ice chunks crumbled off and fell away below us, until we gained the final wind-blasted snow plume leading up to the top of the cornice. It was the unrateable, unknowable aspect of climbing, a blend of faith and balance between life and flying to heaven that made the summit of Changzheng feel so good. We edged back down, hugging the ridge above a broad snow slope that swept back into the Rongbuk Valley. When the snow turned back to rock, we galloped down the mountain and into camp before dinner. Eric would join Mike and me on a foray up on to Everest, but the monsoon snow and a night camping out at 7600 metres (24,934 feet) didn't get us any higher, and with work calling, he headed home to Boulder. And then we were two.

In mid-August we were joined in Advanced Base Camp by a group of Spanish (Catalan) climbers from Barcelona, who became fast friends as we whiled away the days and evenings acclimatising and awaiting good weather. In the group were Araceli Segarra who would go on to climb Everest the next year with David Breashears and the IMAX team and Xavi Lamas, their doctor. Having done medical research in Boston, Xavi's easy command of English saw him wandering over to our camp to share stories in the long evening hours. I had told our tale of climbing Changzheng a few weeks previously and the fun we'd had getting up and down the 1800 metres (5905 feet) of vertical in under 24 hours, good preparation for any of us going onto Everest's North Face and hoping to get up in a couple of days.

With cloudy weather and snow still thick on Everest, the Catalans decided to go up Changzheng as well, following the route Eric and I had taken. We previewed the route for them, the twists, the turns, the uncertainties of the snow and the final hair-raising but spectacular finish. They set out one afternoon to sleep high up on the ridge, go to the summit and come down the next day. They wandered out of camp with the slow steady pace you adopt early on at high altitude and soon climbed up out of sight before appearing on the ridge high above to camp for the night.

We were lazing around camp the next day when the Catalan's Sherpa cook came by my tent.

'Robert — can I borrow your telescope? There has been an avalanche.'

Intermittent radio messages flowed down, transmissions broken up by the ridge, but soon one came through clear enough to learn Xavi had been swept away down the snow slope from high on the peak. The slope had fractured, with all the team except Xavi just above the fracture. The avalanche was huge and swept the whole mountainside away, carrying Xavi over the cliffs and out of sight below them. The avalanche path was obscured by clouds that floated high on the mountain, but from our earlier ascent, I knew the path the avalanche took as it appeared from higher up, disappearing over the cliffs into a hanging, cliff-strewn canyon.

Mike Bearzi and I threw a few things in our packs and walked up the Central Rongbuk above our Advanced Base Camp, then cut straight up into the cliffs, scrambling up steep terraces into the hanging glacier suspended high above. The canyon was narrow, deep and dark, the sun filtering down over the cliffs like rain. It was a small side entrance to the heights that led nowhere, and I doubted anyone had been up here before. It was just one of the thousands of high valleys in the Himalayas that live in perpetual obscurity, leading nowhere important or to peaks too insignificant to warrant ascents. A single gorak appeared, the pure black large raven of the Himalayas, carrier of omens, floating on the winds overhead. The cliff bands rolled back and we surfaced in a rocky bowl, jumbled boulders at the base, with a snow slope leading up steeply again into the heights and the summit of Changzheng far above us. The avalanche had poured over the cliffs, spread out across the snow and then funnelled together at the base.

We saw Xavi's ice axe first, thrown out at the bottom of the avalanche, a convoluted mass of snow blocks packed 5 metres high and 30 metres wide. We looked along the base of the snow and soon spotted a single climbing boot. Only one boot, crampon still strapped tight to it. What violence of snow would tear a tightly strapped double boot from your foot?

We searched further up the snow, with a little hope that perhaps we might even find Xavi alive. Then we had a look up at the expanse of ice blocks and cliff so far above and knew that hope wasn't rooted in the reality of the fall. The gorak circled lower and the chill air of the afternoon rolled off the ice and into the canyon around us. I climbed over the ice blocks in the middle: tumbled, ragged ice that was angrily bunched up, uneven underfoot, ice still shifting and uncertain after its fall from the heights in the clouds above us.

I could see nothing more in the debris, no pack, no articles of clothing and no blood. But the boot and the ice axe below were obviously Xavi's, somewhere in this icy chaos he must be buried. I traversed back and forth, back and forth, climbing slowly up the avalanche.

'He's here Robert, Xavi's here.'

Mike stood unmoving at the side of the avalanche. He didn't move closer and waited for me. I went over and we climbed up to Xavi together.

There was no question he was dead. His body was intact, but bent and twisted in ways not humanly possible, a rag doll tossed out of the ice. We'd rushed out of camp when we had the radio call from the Catalan team climbing above, up through the cliffs and now there was suddenly no need to do any more rushing. We looked down at Xavi, the shape of a human, but with no human life.

'I guess we will need to cover him up,' Mike said.

Mike pulled out his bivvy sack and we moved on to the practicalities of having to touch Xavi. Touching human death makes it very real. In the mountains it is the reality of lifelessness. Moving arms and legs to fit into a linear space and sliding that inside what was no longer a warming bivvy bag but a cold body bag. We straightened Xavi out and slid him into the nylon bag. We dug a trough out of the rocks. Then we laid the bag carefully in that, before piling rocks over the top to protect it from birds.

I noticed we had quit referring to Xavi by name, taking our previous personal relationship we had in camp and casting it aside in order to do what needed to be done for his body. As the sun dived over the ridge and the canyon went suddenly dark and cold, we turned and headed back down the cliffs, along the terraces, back into the green alpine grass tussocks and along the moraine into camp.

Mike and I dropped our gear in our camp and made the very long walk over a very short distance around the lake. I don't think any of the Catalan team expected to hear that Xavi was alive. They had all personally seen the avalanche's immensity and the distance it had travelled from where they stood just above the fracture. But the first real confirmation of any death is always a shock. Our news was received very quietly, the reality confirmed.

Mike and I returned across the lake to our own camp for cups of steaming tea and dinner, then wandered back. There was not much talk, just sitting, I think there was a single malt, and a big emptiness where Xavi's life had been. And the realities of our distance from family and friends and then the need to call Xavi's parents, parents who had lost another son to climbing several years earlier. None of us would love the mountains any less, but the penalties as we climbed higher and higher went up and up. The mountains seemed to give and take instantaneously. One minute a glorious sunrise, the next a friend died. Many climbers didn't have nine lives, some barely seemed to have one.

The Catalan team was highly experienced; they had climbed the South Side of Shishapangma together in a single blast from bottom to top. They were true alpinists and highly talented and experienced mountaineers with a long apprentice in the mountains. And Xavi was their doctor, who had done the hard climbs with them along the way. Then he had lost his brother several years before and had come to Everest not to climb high but to be with and support the team. He was being safe.

Xavi's parents said he should be buried in the mountains, so two days later we climbed back up the hidden valley, around the base of the now melting and seemingly benign avalanche debris, and took the protective layer of rocks from over his body. We moved his body down and tunnelled out a deep grave under a truck-sized rock. Broken clouds floated high overhead, the sun shone, the gorak flew past. The mountain Xavi had been pulled from by the avalanche was now his headstone and the expanse of the West Rongbuk Glacier lay at his feet. On a flat stone was carved in Catalan: 'Xavi Lamas. We will never forget you.'

Someone had some music, we sat in the sun on our rocks and then one by one wandered off down the cliffs and back to camp. The wake went on long into the night, stories, a pause, an occasional translation, a few tears, long hugs good night.

I lay in my tent that night, conversation still drifting across the tiny lake that separated our camp from the Catalans. Being safe in the mountains, the high mountains and it seemed particularly the Himalayas, and specifically Everest, just wasn't really possible.

Three days after the memorial service for Xavi, Mike and I passed the base of the canyon where his body now rested, on our way back up to the North Face. We'd never questioned returning to the mountain after his death, despite the penalties that were ultimate and sometimes completely unexpected. We knew the mountains were dangerous, our belief had been confirmed, we still loved the mountains and wanted to climb to the top of the world. It wasn't heroic in any way, just realistic for a pair of climbers who never really wanted to do anything more than climb. So off we went.

Despite the storms rolling through, this would be our fourth foray that season up onto the North Face of Everest. I'd gone up alone and slogged to a stop at 7600 metres (24,934 feet), the snow going from ankle, to calf to thigh deep. The monsoon had been an enthusiastic one, and it wasn't getting any better. Eric, Mike and I had gone up, climbing through the night to the base of the Great Couloir, camped out for a night, then Eric had gone down, wisely as it turned out, as the additional two nights Mike and I spent camping out got us no higher. The clouds rolled in each afternoon, it snowed, we stomped a few hundred metres up the Couloir and then would retreat, hoping against hope that the snow would harden up, just a bit, and the next day would be better. But it was a fool's game. We were waiting for a monsoon to fade that just didn't want to let go and let us finally climb.

A day after leaving Advanced Base Camp, Mike and I were at our camp on the highest point of the Rongbuk Glacier, lazing away the afternoon in the sun. The weather looked suspiciously good. So that evening, one last time, Mike and I clipped into our skis at 9 p.m., and set off up the hill. In the headlamps, the snow crystals reflected brightly. Outside the circle of our headlamps, nothing existed. Despite the night, the hour, the altitude, senses were tuned to the crevasses, the ever shifting, snowed over, where are they hidden now, crevasses. Hidden inside our down suits we were cocooned from the elements, warm. It felt secure and our breath echoed out in fog clouds. At the base of the first bergschrund, a towering vertical cliff, we cached the skis under the lip and snuck around the end, crampons biting the ice. We swapped our ice axes from hand to hand as the cold ate up into our wrists, one of us leading and breaking trail, then the other.

We didn't use ropes, we didn't have ropes, too heavy, and the safety they provided was more psychological than realistic. We had found climbing alone was also faster; one of us would lead at his own pace, then the second person would follow along until he inevitably caught up in the deep snow, then we traded places. It was 800 vertical metres (2624 feet) to where the immensity of the face merged into the Great Couloir. In the darkness it was surreal, intensely beautiful, yet inhuman, a moonscape set on earth. Eight hours of moving up, seemingly going nowhere, just the occasional look over the shoulder to see the plains of Tibet starting to open up, the light touching the east in the tiniest hints of dawn, of sun, or warmth and a return to reality. We were never more than a few metres apart, and never needed to talk.

We climbed, we stopped and sipped tea, we climbed, we sat in the snow and rested. It was both monotonously boring, physically gruelling and spiritually uplifting to be here at all. Mostly, though, it was just plain hard work, with the niggling worry about the snow, the layers and the hope that the clouds on the plateau stayed on the plateau and didn't roll in our direction tonight. We paused at the ever iconic and welcoming Tombstone rock, glowing dully in the darkness.

As the sun touched the West Ridge far off on our right, we climbed the last hundred metres up to our lonely tent cut in under the rock at the corner of the Great Couloir. It was the one place on the face that could be called a bit safer, a bit flatter and would serve as a camp. The ledge was a couple of metres long and a metre wide, which with a little excavation, served its humble purpose. Tucked in under a rock cliff, it had the slight essence of a cave. It was a hidden haven in the immensity of the North Face and was such a relief from the slope, always falling away, always a place you never wanted to slip and slide off into the space below. It was the same place I'd camped two years before, all alone. Now I was back with Mike, with a partner for the trail ahead.

At four o'clock the next day the early morning ritual was repeated. Best to not think. Altitude headaches, the stove sputtering, headlamps flickering, sliding into damp socks and fat down suits, surrounded by food packets and coffee packs. Everything was frosted over; a touch of the tent created an internal snowstorm. The wind outside was troubled. It swirled. There was no real conversation.

'Hot now.'

'Enough room?'

'Got a spoon?'

Climbing within the mammoth clutch of Everest, existence was simplified. We knew what we had to do and we did it. A simple shared goal, knowledge of exactly what needed to be done. Now it was time to do it. Ours was a symbiotic friendship without any further thought needed, bound by the need to climb higher, to the top of the world.

Our heads eventually popped from the tent. We probably looked like cartoon characters, one of us and then the other emerging. We turned the corner immediately that led up into the Great Couloir, and crabbed upward, searching, always searching for less deep snow. We climbed independently, separate bits of humanity connected only by footsteps linking our progress. The colours of the plateau over 3000 metres below faded slowly into brown, then deep blue and finally a pink haze. Altitude tunnelled our vision into a porthole of clarity, like looking directly from a plane window. Streamers of cloud stretched overhead, heralding an approaching storm. We kept climbing. We had heard reports scratching in across the shortwave radio at Base Camp about the storm and seven deaths far away on the heights of K2. Eight thousand metres allowed us only a snowflake of latitude in any decision. Xavi lurked in our thoughts; it was very easy to cross over from this life. It was direct evidence that the mountain environment could be unkind.

We climbed up through the snow, step by step by step. It varied from calf-deep to knee-deep to thigh-deep snow, when it felt more like swimming. There just wasn't the reprieve that I had two years before on my solo, when sometimes I could actually move up, with hard snow crunching under my crampons. Even with two of us, movement had been effectively stymied. But it was good having a friend, a fellow soul to move up with, to confirm that up was still possible.

At 8000 metres (26,246 feet) the Great Couloir necked down to half its greatness, actually closing down so we could touch the orange and grey rock right alongside us. A cliff band broke the side of the couloir that I'd bivouacked in two years previously, and I suspected from talking with Messner it was where he put his tent on his Everest solo. There certainly weren't many options up here. For a mountain this big you would think there would be a few more places to camp. Mike and I dug and pushed and shoved the snow around until we had a platform nearly flat and nearly as wide as the tent and then stacked it in against the rock. Our altimeter was reading just over 8000 metres and the stove only sputtered to life reluctantly. We were within a very reasonable striking distance of the top. Tired but healthy, camp made and tucked up in our warming sleeping bags. It was close quarters, but it was comfy. If we could keep the headaches at bay and rest, tomorrow the top.

As darkness settled and the stove fizzled out, the cold set in. It went from pretty dark to completely, cannot see anything dark. The gentle patter of snow started. A flake touching the tent here, and then there and then again. Frost built up on the inside when we sealed up the tent. It was frosting the inside as it snowed outside. Accustomed to the solitude and loneliness of soloing, I found Mike's company especially welcome in the overwhelming solitude. I must be fine, there was a great climber who was up here with me who had also chosen to climb high, to keep climbing, to camp out, and to not go down. We warded off thoughts of snow while discussing coffee franchises, pizzas and developing country politics. We looked down the slope and out at Gyachung Kang, the peak just north of Everest, just a few metres off the magic 8000-metre measurement, thus leaving it in obscurity. 'That is where the real climbing is,' said Mike. 'Great ridges, only a few ascents, obscure and beautiful. That is what I want to climb.'

Here we were on one of the best routes on Everest and Mike was dreaming about being over there, on the untracked, untrodden ground, doing an entirely new route on Gyachung Kang. I could understand it, but my heart was all in getting up Everest, in getting to the top of the world. That is what I wanted, maybe all I wanted. Mike was far less concerned with the known, and preferred the unknown, the difficult, the obscure. Big hard climbs that were virtually without names.

We dozed and I silently cursed the snow. All we needed was a bit of luck, a little hard snow underfoot and a little less white stuff falling from the sky: was it too much to ask?

At dawn I crawled out into the snow. It was now thigh deep. We needed a rest anyway. I must have known this was folly, but Mike was happy to stay. 'Maybe it will all avalanche, then we will get a clear run at the top?'

The couloir was thinner up high and it looked possible, rivulets running down the centre, perhaps firming up the snow? We pounded our one piton in and tied off the top of the tent to the cliff. We were just far enough off the side of the couloir to escape any snow slide. With a bit more shovelling, the tent platform was a bit flatter and perhaps more comfortable. The view was good. We were pulled like magnets towards the top. So close. It was Everest, it was worth it. The snow blew itself out in the morning. We crafted a new plan.

It was slow going with the altitude and the snow, but we felt good, one could have even accused us of having fun. We would start at nine o'clock at night. We could climb through the night and the deep snow. We didn't care how slow we climbed; we would just climb. It was less than 800 vertical metres to the summit. We had resolve, we shared a desire, which could have been considered a burning desire, except it was too cold. We had been up high on Everest enough to know we were fine. It was hard, but we were harder, tougher than the mountain and together we would get up this thing. We ploughed a trail out in the afternoon to give us a head start.

At 9 p.m. we exited the tent and crawled out into the middle of the Great Couloir. The moon was a three-quarter crescent, curved over the cliffs at the far side of the shadowed canyon leading towards the summit. The moon arced through the jagged black cliffs, shining without reflection through the towers and cracks. Spindrift snow whirled, circling, dropping into the apex of the Couloir. An eerie darkness pervaded everything, cut with moon-grey shadows. The moon was as much a part of our climb as the earth, connected by the only light we had. The evening wind came up, pushing the snow across the moon in waves, darkness lapping at reality.

Our feet disappeared into the snowy darkness of the steep slope, legs disappearing below the knee. Ice crept out of our crampons, up through our feet and into our legs. Our headlamps wavered upward on the slope, a cold beam of light, alien in the mountain's darkness. Snow rose to our waists and rolled in waves down behind us. There was no more track from whoever led, the snow simply filling in behind the climber in front. We took turns anyway, one taking over as the other faltered. Soon the moon decided even it had had enough. It disappeared behind the cliffs. We struggled on for a few more metres. Looking back, the tent was still in the headlamp beam. We had maybe gone 50 metres in an hour. Maybe that was optimistic. We looked at each other in our headlamp beams. I shook my head. Mike did the same. We didn't need to talk, we were going nowhere, we certainly were not going to the top.

The tent looked forlorn when we reached it. Another night? Better to wait out the night, as 8000 metres is insidious, but it is also beautiful, perhaps the most beautiful view in the world out over the Tibetan Plateau and the morning would give us that sunrise. Besides, if we were to return to normal life, why not sleep at night and not climb it away? So we collapsed and when the shady dawn arrived it was filled with portent and felt ominous. Maybe we had been too high for too long? Maybe we had already died and used up the last of our lives? I was lured in and out of hallucinations. We really had to go down. It wasn't going to be a fast death but a slow one this time it seemed. But even though I had been high for days on end, I still felt marginally strong. Mike and I had been cooking and eating and talking and sleeping like real people. It had been fun.

Our track up had been obliterated in the snow and even the short traverse back out into the centre of the Couloir was a wade out into a seemingly bottomless pit. Turn left, one last look up. But it led nowhere; I couldn't even lift my leg against the snow. So it was down. And down in defeat is a very hard down. Three nights in the heights had pretty much taken all we had and a bit more. But down was down. Foot out, gravity, move forward. Mike moved down quickly and around our camp at the corner of the Great Couloir and disappeared behind the rock outcrop. I came around the corner and he was already a fast 150 metres lower. 'That was quick,' I thought.

Mike waited, sitting expectantly in the middle of the slope.

'Avalanche,' he said.

Aha. I thought he had descended quickly. The soft snow trail was now obvious, the avalanche breaking off at the top of the small bowl above what we now stood in and curling down the mountain before piling up around our feet.

'I just slid down. Bit scary, but fast,' said Mike.

'I stopped, I just stopped,' he said, rather incredulously.

It just seemed a random thing, the level of danger we were used to now included an avalanche Mike had just been in.

Oh well. Off we continued down. We circled the bergschrund at the base of the face and collected our skis. We were still looking forward to the ski. As tired as we were, as weak as the climb had left our legs, we still carved down over the hard snow and over the natural moguls in the snow. The skis skittered and dived and brought us back to our glacier camp, just long enough to pack a few things and float off down the mountain.

The best chance at doing the North Face of Everest, without oxygen and in fine style, was past. But it had been a great season, great climbing, lots of time up high and lots of good times. We'd suffered, but we hadn't died, and we were certainly still friends, very good friends, from sharing a dream and climbing towards, if not to, the top of the world.

Two years later Mike would be back, but this time without me and for an attempt on Gyachung Kang. On an acclimatisation climb on a nearby peak, in the shadow of Everest he would fall to his death. At his memorial service in Boulder, Colorado, attended by hundreds of people, from climbers to people he had done his magical woodworking for, to just acquaintances from Boulder, I learned that while I'd known the Mike who was truly unique and talented in the climbing world, he had a whole raft of people he knew from completely different worlds. His talents as a climber had been balanced with his artistry as a woodworker and carpenter. People knew him from the work he had done on their homes, to bumping into him on his frequent afternoon solos of the Flatirons above his house on the hill.

Mike too had been an avid soloist, a natural lover of high places, with a great talent for movement over the ice and rocks. I didn't feel like he really got his nine lives; it all had ended so suddenly. And my Everest partner was gone, maybe it was time to realise this really wasn't the mountain for me, that my own lives were very close to being used up, if they hadn't been already.

8

EVEREST NORTH RIDGE, WINTER SOLO – LIFE IS LONELY

'Let's go have a look,' I said to Lakpa. 'Just you and me. I want to see what the route is like. Tomorrow, after breakfast.'

'Okay,' he said, 'after breakfast then.'

The night was cold before the sun even set, then the dark came and with no moisture in the atmosphere the stars sat just above the mountain. The Milky Way was a bright swathe like drifting snow across the sky and the moon cast dark shadows. Getting from the cook tent home to my small tent didn't even require a headlamp, as the rocks on the glacier reflected moonbeams. The wind cracked the tent fabric, an incessant snapping sound, guy ropes pulled tight yet still the tent twisted sideways and popped with wayward gusts. It felt impermanent, transitory. We could only huddle and hide, and when we went outside we had to be swathed in down and keep moving or the cold set upon us and crept into our bones in minutes.

At Advanced Base Camp I had one sideways-leaning cook tent. A cook and two Sherpas. I had a two-man tent, stuffed with the warmest down sleeping bag I could find. That was really the only place that was warm. With two hats and a hood the sound of the wind was baffled, and I could retreat and sleep.

There was bright clear light at dawn, but no warmth in the sun. The winter winds ripped over the top of Everest and stripped it clean of snow. The rock was greyer and darker than other times of year, the sun low on the horizon and the long nights holding the cold. Even the crazy but fun dog that had followed me up from Base Camp wasn't happy in the tent alcove any more and whimpered his way into my tent. Any source of heat was good I figured.

Lakpa and I ate breakfast with our gloves on. We were already shivering and had to get moving. Sonam filled us with pancakes and kept the stove roaring after we were done. I could see he had no plans to turn it off. The blue flame was curiously reassuring but provided no heat as the tent was so draughty that any semblance of warmth just disappeared.

'It's colder here than the South Col,' said Sonam. 'A lot colder,' and he rolled his eyes summitwards, a combination of reality and letting me know he thought I was crazy.

It was still possible to warm up a bit when moving, so that is what we did when we left Advanced Base Camp, setting a fierce pace up the moraine. There was still a hint of a trail in place from the autumn climbers, but it didn't really matter, the way was clear, weaving up the glacier. It felt good to be starting the climb. When I'd gotten up in the morning and put all my clothes on and went to pack my pack, I'd realised there really wasn't anything else to carry; I was wearing it all already. I felt the way Ed and Stephen and I had felt setting off on our summit bid on the Kangshung Face — there wasn't really a need for a rope, so thus no harness. And there wasn't a need yet for oxygen. Water not inside a pocket just froze, and I'd already had that problem two days before on the walk up to Advance Base Camp. So there was no need for a pack. It made for a quicker ascent, more fun, just hiking up the hill, unladen and unencumbered.

At the edge of the glacier we paused and put our crampons on. The reassuring snap and thunk of the heel locking in. The dog had come along, he didn't need crampons, he just followed along. I hoped he knew about crevasses. The sun was moving up and yet still had no heat, the actual air temperature was so low even the normally blazing Himalayan sun couldn't seem to do anything about it. I remembered being here in the spring with Paul Teare and Mike Bearzi and it was so hot we wore T-shirts.

The intense cold also made the cold different. It felt dangerous. As if a simple pause, a moment's lapse, any mistake, would suddenly be a very real problem that it would be very hard to escape. Sonam was alone down below huddled in his sleeping bag next to the stove. Lakpa and I above on the route. I hadn't bothered with radios and knew the satellite phone was little more than a weight in the pack so I hadn't bothered to bring it along either. As much as Everest had become popular in all the other seasons of the year, had become a place for a picnic at the end of the Rongbuk road for tourists, in winter we were discovering it was a different world.

The last climbing team had escaped in early October, walking out over the Pang La Pass in a snowstorm. Luckily, the winter winds had swept the road clear again and we had snuck back into Base Camp in early December to the North Side Base Camp. The normal need to get in early and choose a good Base Camp site wasn't of any concern. There was no one there and, over the whole month of December, not a single visitor.

The glacier angled gently uphill; it was good to move across it, finally feeling real warmth from our speed, being able to unzip the down suit just a bit. The warmth flowed out into the legs, warming them at least to the ankles. Applying the crampons had sucked so much heat away, the feet would never fully recover while climbing.

The route to the North Col looked a jumble of snow and ice blocks from below, but the route was pretty clear. Without ropes or people on it, the immense slopes above were virgin and exciting, like picking a new route up an unclimbed face.

From the glacier the slopes steepened abruptly, going from the nearly flat glacier to front pointing up the brick-hard snow. The points bit cleanly, crisp dicing sounds in the cold air. Crisp was good, ridding thoughts of the 'it is just so brutally cold' thinking. Lakpa and I carried a single axe each, and with no packs or ropes we moved effortlessly up the slopes. The sun was high enough, now shooting its rays straight into the slopes so that there was finally a bit of warmth coming through. It was a beautiful winter's day, a great day to be climbing on Everest. The first 100 metres and the initial steep section passed quickly, the muscles warming, the crampon points solid in the snow, a connection to the mountain and on to the heights above. It was good to finally be climbing.

This winter attempt on Everest's North Ridge had been borne out of my experience two years previously, when I had hatched a plan to climb Shishapangma in winter.

Setting our sights on the Shishapangma South Face, we eschewed the normal approach into Tibet and worked out an ascent up through the well-known Langtang area of Nepal, with the route leading us up over a high pass and across the border and down to the route.

Our time on Shishapangma had laid the groundwork for this climb, as I'd realised it was possible to move around the Himalayas in winter. You just had to be perfectly prepared and ready for cold and wind and snow that added a whole different dimension to the experience. The Himalayan winter wasn't just cold, it had temperatures that dipped to a level that were inhumane at times. They were at the outer bounds of human existence. A few seconds of exposed skin and we would get frostbite. At times, the wind was so strong all we could do was hide in the tent and hold onto the poles. But we were rewarded with mountains that were pristine and we were all alone. We had met but a few trekkers lower in the Langtang, and the upper valleys were devoid of people. A lone lodge in the final village was open and we huddled around the stove with the family, endless cups of tea in our hands, as much to drink as to warm our hands.

And my solo ventures high onto the North Face of Everest still resonated with me — there was nothing quite like being alone high on Everest with no one around. And soloing, in a purist sense, was almost impossible as the main seasons had so many people climbing that at some point you would probably end up following a line of footsteps, a rope or, even worse, getting stuck in a queue. That was no way to climb. So the idea percolated up after my climb on Shishapangma that perhaps a winter climb on Everest, from Tibet, would be possible. A quick check with the historian and keeper of the archives of Everest ascents, Elizabeth Hawley in Kathmandu, and it was verified that no one had climbed from Tibet to the summit in winter. She sent me one of her rare and encouraging notes, starting with:

> *Dear Robert Anderson,*
> *It was a pleasant surprise to find a fax from you waiting for me this morning. I have been wondering who would get the clever idea to brave severe winter weather to be the last of one millennium and/or the first of another atop Everest. I might have guessed it would be you.*

I knew that just getting into the mountain could be impossible or involve walking 100 kilometres from Tingri if the Pang La Pass was closed with snow. Tibet in the winter, it started to sound like fun, a real adventure when adventures on Everest were getting harder and harder to find.

With the turn of the century coming up, would it be in any way conceivable to summit Everest on the first day of the new century? I talked to a few sponsors, letting them know there were a lot of unknowns. Even reaching Everest in winter could be impossible. But it was also so far-fetched that a few thought it was worth it. So the money flowed in, tickets were booked and I asked a few of my climbing partners whether they had an interest. Paul Teare, who was normally up for anything, quickly said no.

'Too cold,' Paul said, 'way too cold. And what about the wind Robert? It doesn't even stop blowing in the spring on the North Ridge. What do you think the winter will be like?'

It was true. But I was now committed. And I knew that as much as Everest could be truly impossible at times, maybe there would be a short window, a few days in December when the wind would drop and it would be possible to scamper up the North Ridge. It isn't a long route; I'd soloed up as high as the top camp at 8200 metres (26,902 feet) before when I'd done my new route. The North Ridge seemed well suited to a fast winter solo.

Kathmandu in the winter was a cold, dry city. Tourists were few, many local shop doors were shut against the cold. Dust blew down the deserted streets. The flow of excited trekkers flying in and dirty trekkers returning from the heights was virtually non-existent. It was a local city. I found my two Sherpas and the cook, packed up what we needed, tucked seven bottles of oxygen away in a crate and we drove up to the Tibetan border. The normal streams washing the road away, the tumbling waterfalls dropping from the heights, were all frozen into place. In Tibet, the lush forests we normally ascended through were grey, leafless trees. Hotels were shut and we huddled around fires in small local lodges. My regular Tibetan Mountaineering Association Liaison Officer Tsering was at the border to greet me. 'So good of you to come out yourself to join me,' I said when we settled into the local rice and omelette meal, a small bowl of shelled peanuts on the side.

'Robert, I was the only one who agreed to go. Nobody else was coming out to meet you here in the winter.'

So much for feeling special. It had taken me months of negotiations to secure a winter permit, none having been issued before. Having spent the last fourteen years navigating through the labyrinth of the Chinese

Mountaineering Association and then dealing locally and having many contacts in Tibet, I'd convinced them an Everest winter permit was nothing really different: just change a few months, move dates around and send the people and the trucks out from Lhasa to meet me. I didn't negotiate the fee as I normally did, arguing over every yak and hotel price to get the best deal. I just added it up and wired off the money. I sent the funds well in advance and finally got the permit back from Mr Ying. Tibet, Everest, North Ridge Expedition, headed for the heights. I left any mention of winter off the permit. I just booked it for December/January and left it at that.

The road out of Nepal into Tibet cuts through one of the few gorges to bisect the Himalayan mountains and cross over the Nepali border. Any road that goes through the world's tallest mountain chain is by default going to be through a very deep canyon, and crawling up out of the border town of Zhangmu, you travel relentlessly up for a day and a half to a pass at over 5000 metres (16,404 feet). The walls of the gorge slowly release you from the deep forest, then into scrub and bushes. Then the road leads up into the alpine zone and the windswept heights of the plateau.

I soon realised how lucky I had been, as snowdrifts lined the road, extending up over the sides of the Land Cruiser. Early snows had closed the road, and only a long period of better weather had allowed it to be ploughed out and the border reopened. When we hit the plateau a snow-blasted landscape revealed itself, the road a swathe of black carved into the icy terrain. The Himalayas came up out of the whiteness, shimmering in an icy grey haze. The heater on the Toyota was set to maximum heat and maximum fan. Gusts buffeted us on the open plateau. The adventure had started, and I hadn't even left the car. My Sherpas were stoic. Everest in winter, what did we expect?

Tingri, Tibet. I'd always liked the place for no logical reason. It was high and cold. It was a dump. The food was dubious. The people could be unfriendly. The army base was staffed with young and highly disgruntled soldiers who took the dislike of their posting to the streets by bullying both locals and tourists alike. They threw rocks at the dogs.

Being winter, there was only one small lodge open. My Sherpas and I were all stuck together in a room with no heat. The local Chinese Army officer, though perhaps finding me little more than a novelty, pulled me off into his group and we ate and drank together. The soldiers wore long dark green army coats and big black scarfs, both outside and inside. The stove by late evening glowed red. Inevitably, there would be Tsingtao beer, followed by Maotai, and toasts.

Tingri has the atmosphere of a lawless, wild-west town. Tibetan nomads were camped on the outskirts. Kids wore yak-skin clothing that looked like it had been sown onto them. They played outside, kicking cans and shouting in the wind. Best of all, Tingri was the gateway to Everest. From the hill above, by a fort-like monastery inhabited by a lone monk, you could see the top of the peak. I'd been in Tingri so many times: in the spring before the Kangshung Face, in the summer when we had gone to the North Face, and out again in the autumn when we had left. I knew all the seasons but winter. Now, even the ubiquitous packs of wild dogs had retreated, hiding by the fire in the low earthen houses. People moved from door to door and shop to shop quickly, ducking out of one and following the walls to shield from the wind before dipping into another. Smoke from yak-dung fires permeated the air, thick and then wafting quickly away with the winds and into the grey sky. The villagers were in hibernation.

My liaison officer told me about his retreat from Base Camp in the autumn, snow so deep the Italian team had given up and walked out down the Rongbuk and over Pang La Pass. The team had left gear along the way, barrels tucked away in the lone building and up on the mountain, a stream of equipment abandoned as they had struggled out in the early season snowstorm. Whether we could even get to Base Camp was looking doubtful. In season, the drive would have daily traffic and the drivers knew every washout and pothole. In the winter, they had disappeared from the roads altogether.

The road up off the Tibetan Plateau goes up nearly a 1000 vertical metres, negotiating 40-plus switchbacks as it carves its way up the hill to the 5200-metre (17,056-feet) Pang La Pass. The seat in the Land Cruiser was low on padding: too many miles on too many rough roads for too many years. At some point it had been recovered in a cotton gingham that wasn't standing the test of time. Even the Land Cruiser was bowed by the altitude and we crawled up the final few feet to the top of the pass at a yak's pace.

In winter the Tibetan air has a clarity, a pureness that renders the sky a perfect shade of blue. The streamer off Everest wasn't the typical moisture-filled plume of other seasons; it was a streamlined vapour trail, thinly twisting and formed by the jet stream. Everest was so high that its connection was closer to the sky above than to the earth below.

The light brown of the hills in front of Everest was intense, in contrast to the snow of the lower peaks, with the stark and perfect outline of Everest set against the sky in the background. Everest was framed by the world's fifth-tallest peak, Makalu, on the left. On the right was the sixth-tallest peak, Cho Oyu. It was a perfect, radiant day, with a clarity I'd never experienced before on my many trips over the pass. Perhaps it was a good omen, a good sign. I'd take anything, as I well knew the odds were not good for going far, as much as I felt even a small chance was worth the journey.

Tibet. Everest. Winter.

What adventurer wouldn't want to go? Even Elizabeth Hawley had a rare moment of enthusiasm: 'That would be a very noteworthy climb,' she commented as I finished filling out her form when we met in Kathmandu. 'Do come and see me on your return. I'm not exactly busy this time of year,' she had said as she farewelled me from the city.

The drop off the Pang La was frightening, 1000 metres of vertical descent, dropping down the other side of the pass with the engine turned off to save fuel, the heater fan churning cold air from the vents, the driver wrestling the suddenly unpowered steering around the switchbacks. It was easy to feel that dying long before getting to the mountain was a distinct possibility.

The Rongbuk Monastery had a single stream of smoke coming from the monk's quarters. No yak-herders camped in the courtyard and no children played along the road. The driver pointed at me to hold the door when we stopped, so the wind howling past wouldn't rip it off. Dirt and stones flew through the air. We paused only long enough to see there was no one wanting to venture out, and then bumped and bounced the last few kilometres up the hill to Base Camp.

One low stone building was set below the small ridge and the Mallory memorial stone. Inside it was an ice box. It had three rooms, boarded-over windows and was lightless and lifeless. One night inside was all I could take, and I moved out into the comforts of my tent. The next day, a surprisingly healthy dog appeared and took up residence with me, good company in my lonely sojourns around camp.

As part of my Chinese Mountaineering Association contract, I'd had to hire three yaks. So rather miraculously, up the Rongbuk they trundled two days later, with two yak-herders to keep each other company and the yaks moving. I hiked out of camp alongside them, filled with misplaced enthusiasm for the walk up to Advanced Base Camp. But my yaks soon stranded out, burying their hooves deep in the snow drifts and the yak-herders dumping the loads, turning around and heading home. A few more Chinese yuan weren't going to get them any higher. Yaks are not good in snowdrifts between boulders when they can't see where their hooves will ultimately rest.

My liaison officer let me know that was it, the snow was too deep, it was too cold, the Tibetans didn't understand our wanting to climb even in the summer. In the winter it was obvious I was just plain crazy. They had done what they could, got paid and went home.

The next day the Sherpas and I headed up the Central Rongbuk, around the corner into the East Rongbuk and up the glacier. I was very glad to have my Sherpas, load carrying up the Rongbuk Glacier would have been a very lonely business. While we didn't talk much, sharing out the loads, cooking dinner, curled up together in our one tent, at least had the warmth of humanity about it. It had been hard to find Sherpas who were interested in this venture, and with just two it wasn't going to be a lot of fun for them. And I didn't want them to really climb, just help me get into position, get me up and set in Advanced Base Camp so I was within striking distance of the summit.

Day two we moved on up to the corner camp below the ridge on Changtse, leaving the earth below and camping on the glacier. The sky came down grey on our heads. The wind not strong, but biting. There weren't even any of the ubiquitous goraks flying about. Above, the winds curled off the ridges in rotors, pulling the snow up into the sky and then it disappeared. I felt it was a new place I'd never been before, a mountain impossible to imagine. This was the real Everest, devoid of people and life. As much as so many of us managed to crowd the slopes in season, this was a very different place, as remote and inaccessible as any place on earth. I really liked it, this being alone with Everest.

We left our loads at Advanced Base Camp before noon the next day. The emptiness felt strange, a camp on Everest devoid of people. Above, over the North Ridge the summit was just visible. The plume wasn't wafting, it was a direct straight line of cloud, a jet stream of air with none of the floating, wisping sense one got in other seasons. No, this time of year Everest was serious.

We retreated to Base Camp, to pretend to warm up, to eat more, to let the altitude enhance our lungs. I climbed above camp every day, acclimatisation settling in and the feeling of zooming up 1000 metres above camp as fast as I could, a welcome respite from the wind in the afternoon and the long dark nights. The dog always came with me. He didn't beg, he didn't howl, there was no whimpering. It was a simple companionship. When I'd stopped to rest, he would stop to rest. At the summits he looked around, perhaps also admiring the views. Back in the tent at night I read a book and then another, a grey storm blew in and over. Then it was back to the heights, back to make a more serious attempt on the mountain.

The second time up the East Rongbuk we didn't need to camp on the way up the glacier; we were acclimatised, we knew the exact way.

Knowing the trail, we naturally paced ourselves up the track. Normally you would do it with a light pack, but as our camp was being stocked by just us three, that was not the case. I packed extra rice, an oxygen bottle, more bags of tea, Cup-a-Soup sachets and chocolate bars. It was so cold that most of the clothes we had we were wearing, and warming up while walking just didn't really seem to happen.

The trail from Base Camp was crunchy with ice, the rivulets and streams that prevailed in the autumn all frozen hard. The earth was dry, the rocks frosted over. The sound was different, there was no give in the earth, just a cold hard dryness underfoot. At the entrance to the East Rongbuk it was easy to see why Mallory's early expeditions failed to find the way. It is a diminutive cut in the valley wall, at least compared to the rest of the Himalayas. Looking up it, you can't see the curve around the corner and how it leads back up to Everest. Even now it felt like a hidden gateway, a way to sneak right up under the mountain, to reach Advanced Base Camp at 6340 metres (20,795 feet) with little more than a stiff hike. In any season besides winter, yaks will carry your gear up, so dome tents, camp chairs and thick sleeping pads are the norm. When you carry your own gear, none of that is happening.

This was it then, I was going up the hill to solo Everest in winter. I was taking it one loose, rocky step at a time. I watched my feet, rocks set precariously on ice and imbedded gritty grey sand. The pack towered over my head. The wind was slow and strong, coming down the glacier, into my face. I was very alone, but not lonely. The Sherpas were behind me; I'd started right after breakfast and gone out ahead. They weren't overly enthusiastic. Understandably. To get anywhere, or encourage them, I needed to go first, to show I was serious.

I was serious, but not foolish. I knew I'd go as high as I could. I was very much just happy to be here, to have the mountain to myself, to feel this raw cold and sense of power emanating off Everest that was unique to winter. The rest of the year, fine — allow a bit of human habitation. In winter, Everest was Everest, truly Everest.

There was a final hill up the glacier before Advanced Base Camp. It was cut by ageing crevasses, half filled in with rocks, but still with gaping holes to weave around, reminding me of the moving ice underfoot. Then the curve of the final corner and onto the plinth of the glacier where the camp sat, a lowly single camp tent and my own sleeping tent.

We settled back into Advanced Base that evening, with a simple 'we will go have a look' tomorrow at the North Col.

So Lakpa and I climbed up above Advanced Base, to explore the slopes the next day. Once we had done the first 100 metres of steep climbing, we were already high over the glacier. The freedom of climbing unroped, of moving independently, made it fun, the focus on the climbing and not the equipment or another partner. Lakpa and I just climbed, one first, then the other, then sometimes alongside. At the base of the steep slope below, my dog sat, peering up expectantly.

Above the initial steep section up to the North Col, the slope rolled back. This is where Hans Kammerlander had carved his best tracks down from the North Col when I had climbed up with Paul Teare on our previous summit attempt. It was also where the first deaths on Everest had occurred, six Sherpas being carried away in 1922, pulled down and buried in an avalanche. The innocuous nature of the slopes made it easy to be pulled upward onto the mountain, hungering for the heights above and ignoring the dangers below.

The snow stayed hard, crisp, the sun warming for the first time, radiating directly onto the slopes. Being in the lee of the North Col, there was no wind. Lakpa moved ahead across the slope, where the gentle rising ramp faded and we would need to cut left onto the snowy terraces and climb into the seracs, the blocks of glacial ice, above.

There was an obvious transition point, a move from ramp to serac-covered slope, a break in the snow slope, stepping right to left. Lakpa was just ahead, the way was clear, he stepped into the gap, and his leg disappeared, then the edge collapsed as if in slow motion. He threw himself forward over the gaping hole. His ice axe went into the snow above and he pulled himself up and out of the crevasse.

He took two steps higher; the snow was hard again. I just stood there waiting, my heart suddenly pounding, the air silent, the hole revealing a blue-iced crevasse curving off into the depths.

'I fell in,' Lakpa said loudly and breathlessly. We just stood there.

'I fell in, I really fell in,' Lakpa repeated, incredulous he was still on top after feeling the snow bridge over the crevasse collapse.

'You okay?' I asked.

More silence. With mountain accidents you expect there should be a fanfare, a loud noise, a crescendo, a big cavalcade of snow. This had nothing, just a hole, now looking suspiciously small, the size of a big boot.

I edged over. The crevasse was deep and blue and a body-width across, twisting out of sight into the depths of Everest. It was another world Lakpa could have fallen into and disappeared below.

Lakpa looked up from his now solid stance and waved his arm and started climbing again, upward.

'Okay,' I thought. 'Up we go.' And I leapt over the hole, sunk my axe on the far side and stepped up after him.

I remembered Messner had fallen in here too, on his solo. I suspected it was exactly the same place. It was the obvious route, a major feature that wouldn't change and a crevasse that probably lived permanently under the snow here, separating the ramp below, pulling away from the steeper ice above, almost a bergschrund but in the middle of the face.

Messner had completely fallen in, though, landed 10 metres down, and climbed out the other end. Then he continued his solo, probably as close as he would come to dying on the route. His was the first and last real solo on Everest, and something like a little crevasse fall wasn't going to stop him. I was glad Lakpa was undeterred. A hundred metres higher I caught up with him. His eyes still looked a bit big and round.

'You okay?' I asked again. He nodded. 'I fell in,' he repeated. 'I really could have fallen in.'

'Okay, though?' I repeated. I really wanted something more than just heading up the hill, a bit of a we are in this together, or onwards and upwards.

'It's okay,' he said. 'It's okay Robert, we can go to the Col,' almost consoling me. He knew that scouting the route out to the Col was important to me; we had talked about it. Reaching the North Col was the gateway to the heights.

So I stepped out in front and broke trail, weaving up through the seracs, a piece of rope or two occasionally popping out of the ice and disappearing just as quickly. Towards the top we had two sections of steep climbing, fun icy seracs to clamber up and over, climbing together but moving separately, a team but on our own. Just below the Col a steep step rose up. I reached my ice axe up and sunk it in over the top and stepped out onto the North Col.

The North Col is flat, expansive and solid. The view, suddenly opening up across the whole North Face of Everest, is immense, curving around the face and over the West Ridge to frame Nepal and the mountain ranges extending forever into the distance. Seven thousand metres (22,965 feet) was high enough on Everest for me to feel tall, to feel big. Then there was that additional 1800 metres (5905 feet) of vertical up to the summit. The wind immediately went from non-existent to a steady, stiff gale, and the wind-chill plummeted. Lakpa came up and in the expansiveness of it all, in the aloneness of it all, we had a big hug. It seemed a real climb, though it really was to almost nowhere, just a singular place, on a big mountain, in the winter, in Tibet.

The Everest atmosphere was overwhelming, of a mountain complete in itself, devoid of humanity. We were the only climbers on the peak, north or south. We could also well be the highest people on earth right now. Braving the crevasse had reminded us of the immediate dangers, the chance that one step could be a step from this life to the next. It had given us a mountain that was all our own. Not even on the Kangshung

Face had I felt this sense of power from a space on earth. Everest truly reigned supreme.

It was midday. The climb felt big, but the time was small, as we hadn't left until after 9 a.m. It was faster than I had ever come up to the North Col. And certainly more fun.

The route above was windswept and clear; it would be fast climbing above. But even now, up above the last camp below the ridge, the wind was ripping across the snow, and then over the ridge. We could hear it, a background roar of power. It had been that way since we arrived. I wondered if it ever dropped. It must, but how would I know? How to wait and gauge it right? There would be a lot of luck. Should I go down and turn around and come right back up? Retreat to Base Camp and try to time the winds? My Sherpas just wanted to go home; I knew that. Would they be willing to carry another load up to Advance Base Camp if we went down again? Our camp was set, but we needed food to stay, and fuel. There was no water trickling down from anywhere, it was all ice and all that needed to be melted. Too many questions, too many unknowns.

I walked out across the Col to look down the Central Rongbuk, where I had first been when we attempted the North Face Super Couloir. High out on the face were the terraces where Jay and Mark, Harry and I had bivouacked on our tiny ledges before the snowstorm and our lucky slide back down the hill in the morning. The Great Couloir was also so close, the huge slopes leading into it, the distinctive tombstone rock set in the middle and then the long arc over to the mini-camp Mike Bearzi and I had used where the Couloir pinched down.

Way across was the West Ridge Direct where Jay Smith and I had climbed up through the Yellow Band and below the Grey Band, when our oxygen hissed out and we were forced to retreat.

Now I was here again, yet again. I wanted to just keep going. The ridge above always seemed so close. I had been up this way both with Paul Teare and on my earliest solo attempt. It was a fun route, a beautiful ridge to scramble up.

It was too cold for reveries and plans now. The wind howled over the Col, funnelled between the North Ridge and the slopes of Changtse behind us. I spun around for a last look, a last breath taking it all in, and we set off back down the slopes.

Without ropes, we didn't have to worry about clipping and unclipping or anchors, we just climbed down. We knew where the crevasse was and leapt across, back to the ramp, then down the final steep section, cautious until the end. Then we galloped back to camp, the whole descent taking less than an hour. Sonam had seen us coming and the soup was steaming hot, the cook tent further fortified with ice chunks at the base to keep the wind out.

I hadn't realised how cold I was, how four and a half hours out at that altitude and in the winter cold had chilled me through. Lakpa and I were smiling, though, happy, relating the climb to Sonam. The crevasse step was further dramatised, the hole bigger, the slip further, the depths blacker. In reality, it was very close to having been a life-ending moment for either of us. If I had gone first, I would have probably stepped the same way, as it was logical to follow that route and take that exact step. Would I have pulled myself forward as quick as Lakpa and escaped the depths? Not a thing to think about, but I did that night, lying back alone in the warm sleeping bag, in my tent, the wind roaring its crescendo high above. Falling in that crevasse would have been very unpleasant, a very cold way to leave this life behind.

The dog woke me up. Nose in my ear. Trying to warm up. Understandable, as even inside the tent it was horrifically cold. Being in a sleeping bag that rose nearly to the tent ceiling was definitely preferable to being a thin Tibetan dog. I put on my down suit and wore it to breakfast.

We huddled around the stove burner as wind flapped the cook tent. There wasn't much talking; morning coffee and then a welcome round of pancakes ensued. It was too cold to hang out, there was no such thing as a rest day. The altitude meant we were above anything that could be considered a resting place, and the cold sapped energy. I wasn't ready to go down, but to make an attempt we needed more supplies here and I needed more oxygen for the heights. I'd justified using oxygen this time to climb as winter was so much colder. And there was the chance that changes in atmospheric pressure in the winter would potentially make Everest feel even higher. It was high enough already.

So a retreat to Base Camp was pretty inevitable. As much as my heart was pulling me up, the need to get things in place and regroup pulled me back down the hill.

The way down was long, hard and fast, with dinner back in the comparative warmth now of the Base Camp Hotel. We watched a movie, a rerun of *Titanic*, perhaps not the best choice.

Morning. Suitably grey. No wind, but no summit in sight. Into my down suit and over to breakfast. The dog joined me, part of the team.

I opened the heavy door and sat on the side of the yak blanket in our dining room, which was also the kitchen, and where the Sherpas slept.

'We'd like to go home, Robert.'

They certainly had a point there. I was still half and half, still pulled up, thinking that with quite a large dose of luck over the next week, at some point there had to be a break in the weather. I also knew that having watched the weather since I'd arrived in Tingri, it was pretty unlikely. But I wouldn't mind if Everest surprised me.

I knew the Sherpas had well and truly had enough. There wasn't the normal camaraderie with a bigger team, a warm cook tent to while away the evening hours, a team slightly larger than me and my dog. This was 'brutal', as Paul Teare liked to comment about Everest. Everest in winter was Everest squared. The winter, while thinking it was hard, was also frighteningly, mentally daunting. In other seasons it was liveable, even comfortable. In winter there was never a chance to relax or have anything approaching a rest. The tiniest of mistakes, a slip, a bump, a change of weather had an immediate effect. Just living here day to day we were on the edge. The Sherpas repeated how it was harder being up at Advanced Base than even being at the South Col in the regular season, 1000 metres (3280 feet) higher. What would it be like at the top? I had to agree, and we had not yet managed more than two nights at Advanced Base Camp. Staging a climb from above Base Camp would be impossible; it really needed to be done using Advanced Base as a simple stopover, another fast camp on the way up the hill. There was no way to stay there more than a night or two.

I sipped my coffee. I had many reasons to go home, a small sliver of hope in staying and making a real attempt.

My Sherpas waited expectantly. My liaison officer Tsering came in. I knew the minute I mentioned leaving to him we would be gone; he had been making leaving noises since the night we arrived. We would walk around camp in the mornings together with him looking at the sky and the road and him saying, 'Any snow, and the road is closed. It won't open again until March then, you know.'

The crevasse was hovering at the side of my thoughts, the vision of Lakpa lurching downward and then leaping forward to safety. Me looking into the depths, imagining myself there. That would have not been a pleasant use of one of my lives, not at all. The bowels of Everest would not be a place you would want to get stuck and die. There was luck and then there was just being stupid, and I tried not to be that.

I thought back to the North Col. To the simplicity of the climb up, moving quickly and freely up the ice. On the North Col it had been as good as a summit. Maybe that would have to be it, that was the high for the expedition, a solo, albeit a duet with Lakpa and me up to the heights.

The vision of the top from the North Col, that clarity of the North Face set in the amphitheatre above the immensity of the Central Rongbuk, the streamer of air roaring straight off the top. Maybe it was a summit without touching the top, at least for me.

For now, that would have to do.

EVEREST SOUTH COL – LIFE IS POWER

Could this be it? Was I really, actually, finally, going to make it?

I didn't want to believe it until I was there, totally there. After all the expeditions, and all the lives, I just didn't trust even having to make one step more to the top of Everest.

The very last metre on Everest is a small rise, a tiny step up, a clamber onto a tabletop slab of snow. Then I was there, standing on top of the world. And it felt all of that. I was alone, Sibusiso and David still coming up behind me. A slow turn revealed the whole world. I felt as connected to the sky above as the earth below. The wind rippled but didn't push me over. I could stride the few metres from one end to the other and back again. I was truly, literally and figuratively on top of the world.

Sibu came up, with a big hug. And then David. Just us three, alone on top. Sibu pulled out his flag. David did the honours with photos, my camera frozen in a blob in its case. Then we just sat, taking in the view, taking in the whole wide world. It was even better than I expected, and even better being with friends. Just below us, Passang, climbing along with Fred, came up along the ridge. Fred stopped below and Passang came along and joined us on the top. Another hug, more big smiles, more joy.

And now, oh so reluctantly, we had to go down. The climb up had gone so well, well timed, well climbed, some wind, but endless sun. It was perfect. And with a bit of luck, we would be back down in three hours.

Sixty horizontal metres and just a bit down from the summit of Everest on the Southeast Ridge we had passed a final rib of fractured grey rock sticking up above the snow. When I looked down, I saw Fred was still standing there. He had been climbing with us up to the Hillary Step, making good time, and then was just a bit behind us as we crossed over from the top of the Hillary Step to the summit.

He had stopped just this tiny bit below the summit, unmoving. He was so close to the top we could see him clearly from where we stood. David and Sibu and I had waved our arms and shouted, 'Come on up, you are there.'

I came down from the summit, the ease of going down, of movement without having to step up, was so easy after the relentless climb. When I reached Fred, I saw his oxygen mask pushed sideways on his face. His goggles, iced over, were pushed up onto his forehead. We were in the small alcove formed by the rock, the cornice hanging out over Tibet and the Kangshung Face behind us. In front, the whole world. The view over Nepal extended forever and ever.

'Let's go,' I said. 'I'll go back up to the top with you.'

'Robert, I can see the summit, but it is so bright I can't really see it at all,' said Fred, yelling into my ear.

I looked at his eyes, dark and a bit wild and not focusing. I rejected the thought he was only able to register light and dark. We were as close to the top of the world as you could be without summiting. And we were as far from anything known as safety as you could possibly be. It was not a place you would ever want to be without being able to see clearly. Maybe things were a bit hazy for him? But not being able to see what we were climbing? I didn't want to think about it.

'I have to go down,' Fred repeated.

I was still standing expectantly; he could feel it. I was ready to turn and march right back up to the top. I wanted him to summit and I wanted to go back up. This was what guiding was about, helping people get up mountains. And helping people up Everest was the biggest guiding job of all. Here I was, the first time to the tip-top of Everest. One more person up would just be that much better.

'I'm going down now,' said Fred.

'You need your goggles!' It was dawning on me we weren't going up. We were going down. Fred's face was icy. I realised that his normal confidence had faded. Fred was the most experienced climber on our team: he had done more 8000-metre peaks than any of us, he was a natural in the mountains with a huge reserve of skills. Suddenly, that reserve was very important. We had to go down. Getting up seemed easy compared to this. I'd reached the top, but reaching the top isn't much when you are guiding. Getting up and down safely is what you do. It is the one and only objective. If you don't do that, summiting just isn't what you do.

Was this final climb of Everest, this ninth life about to be taken back? I never trusted anything with Everest. I knew how easy it could all change. Poof. Just like that. Summit and die. Not dramatic, factual. Everest just doesn't play games.

And now my joy in finally reaching the summit of Everest was in very real danger of being taken away. When it had really all started so innocently and gone so well, right from the start. It wasn't just my nine lives, now it was somebody else's.

After my winter solo on Everest, I wasn't resigned, but the burning desire to go and touch the top of the world, to have that final few steps completed, just wasn't there. For too many years and so many times I'd circled Everest. From the West Ridge Direct to the Kangshung Face, to the North Ridge and the North Face. To different routes and different teams and every season imaginable. Maybe, just maybe, I was not destined to climb Everest.

And I had a job, a very good job, having moved back to New York from the Far East, working first at advertising agency Ogilvy and then being recruited to join FCB, working just across from Grand Central Station in Manhattan. Our spacious apartment on the Upper East Side looked out over the river. The sun rose and swept across the terrace and lit up the space like a high camp on Everest, just a bit more comfortable. My exercise was running the loop in Central Park, pushing my four-year-old son Myles in a mountain buggy stroller, and running the New York Marathon with my clients.

My daughter Phoebe's words still echoed in my head from the times I went away to the Himalayas and returned to ask how she was doing and she would look me in the eye and say, 'Too long Daddy, too long.'

Everest and the Himalayas were always on my mind, though. Lectures at The Explorers Club and at an Everest symposium at the Smithsonian in Washington DC kept the mountain never far from my thoughts. After a talk I had shared with Stephen Venables, 'spouting' as he called it, about our Kangshung Face climb, he emailed me: 'I've just been invited to guide Shishapangma, but I'm busy — you interested?' He put me in touch with Steve Bell and Simon Lowe at Jagged Globe.

I had never guided before. The idea of waiting for and looking after other climbers was the antithesis of my go fast, go with a small team of talented and experienced climbers, don't use oxygen and, preferably, do a new route interest and ethos. Guiding seemed very much the opposite to that. Looking after other climbers? Being patient? That would be a bit much to expect from myself.

But Shishapangma was very tempting. The only 8000-metre peak wholly in Tibet. I had passed it many times on my way to Everest — it was a gorgeous peak, rising high over and shimmering above the Tibetan Plateau. Maybe the guiding part would be okay? It was a small team of six and Jagged Globe, with a climbing heritage, had a history of attracting strong climbers. My winter climb with Mike Bearzi on Shishapangma was still one of my grand and obscure adventures that, with border considerations, we could never talk about. Shishapangma, and returning to a different side, traversing in from Tibet, held a strong allure.

So I did it, travelling to the UK, picking up a shoe box full of money and flying off to Nepal and on to Tibet. Two weeks after arriving at Base Camp, I called Jagged Globe: 'We are heading home.'

'Oh, sorry to hear that, how high did you get?'

'The top,' I said. 'We already summited and will be back in Kathmandu in two days.'

We had arrived in Tibet in perfect weather and it had stayed that way. So I had everybody up pre-dawn every day in timings that would have even impressed Stephen Venables. It was the post-monsoon season and I was convinced the weather just wouldn't last. Not knowing it wasn't really the way to guide, I'd approached Shishapangma like one of my own climbs, skipping high camp and topping out with my clients, without using oxygen, all in two weeks.

I decided I liked guiding, really liked it. All the logistics, the permits, the sponsorship was pretty much covered. Jagged Globe had been running expeditions for years and the infrastructure, their Sherpa team and support from Sheffield in the UK where they were based all worked. I just had to pack my own gear, get the background on the team and go climb the mountain. Most of the clients were experienced, fun and just wanted to climb.

Maybe we weren't doing new routes, but as long as I could climb peaks I hadn't climbed before and visit new areas it was a great adventure. And helping others with all I had learned was very rewarding. I knew I could climb the peaks myself. But could I help another ten people of widely varying abilities, culture and interests also summit safely? That was the real challenge.

Six months after guiding Shishapangma, I followed it up by successfully guiding Cho Oyu, the world's sixth highest peak. Climbing again without oxygen and skipping high camp, we summited in a single long day from Camp 2. My approach assuredly wasn't for everybody, but the teams were good climbers who could move light and fast up high, without all the detritus of high camps and oxygen masks blocking their view. Cutting out high camps eliminated a lot of the weather risk and the added time at altitude that was often the root cause of failure on many expeditions. Of course, you had to be fit and fast, but on the normal routes on an 8000-metre peak, they just weren't that difficult.

Life went on in New York, work was fun and so were my little kids. Then one crisp autumn day I was sitting in my office in New York City. Out the window the Chrysler Center building glowed from across the street. The email pinged: Steve Bell from Jagged Globe in the UK.

'Do you want to guide Everest for us next year?'

You would think after all the time I had spent on Everest there could be a clear thought, a contemplative moment, a weighing of considerations.

But no. Like so many people, my response was a completely visceral, illogical, non-contemplative, 'Yes.' I was a climber. I climbed big mountains. And the plan for that year made it much more interesting.

It would be the fiftieth anniversary of Ed Hillary and Tenzing Norgay's first ascent of Everest. It was the South Col, which in all my previous eight attempts I'd never done. We had ten clients, and we would have two guides. We had a large trekking group going up with us, and a few more joining us during the season. And to cap it off, a BBC film crew would be coming in towards the end of the season. It would be a mix of the historical fiftieth anniversary, with a big dose of teamwork, organisation and leadership that was not dissimilar to what I did in my business life every day. And, of course, it was climbing Everest via the classic route.

The first hurdle was my very well paid and fun job. I decided to approach it the same way I approached potential sponsors, starting at the top. I scheduled a meeting with our Global Chairman and CEO of FCB, Brendan Ryan. The lure of Everest, of the adventure, fortunately appealed to him. He gave me the two months off work. He paid me. He kept my rather large life and health insurance policies active. Never underestimate the power of Everest.

So here it was, Everest yet again, but in completely changed circumstances. The fiftieth anniversary had focused the world's attention on Everest. My photo of Ed Webster climbing out of the crevasse featured on the cover of *National Geographic Adventure*. No less than 35 teams were signed up for Everest, with a good 441 people registered to climb. Over 80 members of a Nepali/Indian team would be heading up the mountain.

In the Base Camp I had first visited in 1985, as Liz Hawley would write later, 'there are a satellite communications hub, a few cafés and, briefly, a massage parlour'. At times, with trekkers, climbers, Sherpas and journalists, it went from feeling like a village to being more of a city. With the numerous Buddhist shrines, chortens, stacked two storeys high with flagstones and streaming with prayer flags, it was a bright and shining metropolis. The need for electrical power to run everything from battery-charging stations to the larger expeditions' theatres and nightly movies, ensured that generators hummed from every camp. At least one expedition seemed to be celebrating something at some point in time, with the attendant laughs, loud talking and voices raised in song. Nobody was going anywhere near Everest for a wilderness experience.

We had our own big team too, with lots going on. The press, from *Ad Age* in New York to the BBC, wanted to talk to me. As I was guiding, I felt I had to use oxygen; I needed to be able to think. And, hopefully, in joining the masses I'd finally actually be able to make it. That would be nice.

Was I compromising all ethos, though: the climb fast, climb free, climb new, that I had always loved? And using oxygen? That didn't seem to matter so much any more. I loved guiding; it would get me back to Nepal — I wouldn't even have to quit my day job. Downside minimal.

Upside Everest. Maybe this was the way to get to the top? To worry less about myself and more about others. So off I went.

Our team was a United Nations of climbers. Borge Ousland, the renowned polar explorer from Norway. Peggy Foster, who I'd climbed a new route with on Vinson in Antarctica, was attempting to finish the Seven Summits and become the first Canadian woman to climb them all. Kiek Stam from the Netherlands and Rodrigo Limon and Alejandro Garibay from Mexico. Sibusiso Vilane was attempting to become the first black African to summit. And Fred Ziel, an American doctor, with four 8000-metre peaks already completed.

David Hamilton was along to help me guide and we had a strong and talented team of Sherpas I'd worked with before on Shishapangma and Cho Oyu. The stage was set; what could go wrong?

We left the South Col at 9 p.m. on our first attempt, following a conga line of headlamps.

The wind was howling, the tents flapping incessantly as we closed the doors, a repetitive whipping of nylon on rock amplified by the dark. Crampons, already strapped on in the confines of the tent alcove, burned icy through the soles of my boots, like standing on a frozen lake in bare feet. Swaddled in down, the inner man was far from the outer reality, like a space suit separating the human core within from the inhuman world outside.

Tripping, shuffling, ice axe banging my leg, we set off. The 'we' was 130 climbers. The dream was the top of the world. A hundred metres from camp we left the rock pile for the ice. Our group of eight, plus seven Sherpas, was already dispersed, some just ahead, some behind. In the darkness, oxygen masks on, voices muffled through rubber and lost in the wind, we moved upward. The ice steepened, fractured, a thin line was grabbed, the terrain not steep enough to really need it, but steep enough and slick enough that a fall would result in a slide of over a kilometre back into the glacial valley of the Western Cwm. At the end of the thin white rope, a single ice screw stuck out at an oblique angle, shining dully in the glare of my headlamp. It wasn't the kind of protection you would normally trust with one person's weight, while below me stretched a line of people all hauling themselves up the rope. This was Everest, and right now it didn't bear thinking about.

The ice relaxed. The rope ended. Turned loose from a finite connection, dots of light inched across the snow slope and up the hill. I was too hot to move. The roar of the wind inside the tent at the South Col, the biting cold on exiting, had encouraged us to wrap up tightly. Encased in a down suit the size of a sleeping bag, exercise had created a furnace with no vent holes. I was about to expire in the minus 25°C (−13°F) temperatures from the heat. Hat off, neck open, fog rushing up to obscure my vision, I steamed like an overheated car.

Across the snow slope the line snaked and then we headed up the slope, the increasingly steep slope. This was really Everest, the summit night. Don't think too much, just climb.

We were in one of those horrible conga lines that you get in a nightclub when everyone has stayed too long, drunk too much and decides to line up and hold the hips of the person in front of them. Once we were out of camp and on the fixed ropes, it was impossible to pass. It was simply clip and edge and clip and edge upward. There was no sense of pace, simply following steps. Oxygen wraps you up in a world of hissing air, foggy glasses and an inability to see your feet.

The last time I had been up here there had been no trail, no ropes and no one in sight beyond my climbing partners Ed and Stephen. We had no packs, no oxygen. Now we had everything and it was too much. It wasn't even climbing, just a staircase of steps leading alongside a rope, passing anchors and moving up into the steps of the person in front as they vacated their space. At the anchors, the ropes were tied directly into pitons slammed and bent into the fractured rock. At one point, an ice stake had been pounded upward into the rock. I couldn't understand why it was holding weight at all.

The wind, a troubling, ruffling charging beast when we left the Col, kept building. The weather forecast was good; the reality was a building storm. Snow started to drift into the steps as we climbed through the fractured rock bands leading to the Balcony. By midnight it was a howling, twisting maelstrom. Everybody was still heading up, into the dark, into the wind, into the building snow.

Then the first person passed me headed down. Some had just unclipped and clumped down next to us. Others were attempting to clip and unclip around us. With the oxygen masks over our faces, the dark, and a multitude of languages being uttered, there was no real communication. The descending climbers became more of a wave. I was wary of turning back too soon. The nightly breezes could come up and fade just as quickly. If a whole bunch of people turned back, we would finally have the way clear and could get moving.

Finally, I had a hurried conversation with another climber descending. He came out of the darkness with a simple confidence in his step, an ice axe in his hand and comfortably descending off the rope — perhaps a good source of information?

'It's worse, way worse at the Balcony and above,' he said, twisting his mask sideways so I could hear him. 'Not worth climbing higher. It is only getting worse.' And off down he went.

David and I looked at each other; we didn't need to talk. We turned the group around and down we went. Down, down, down, in and out of the South Col and all the way back to Camp 2. Maybe we could come back, maybe we could try again. Right now, we weren't going any higher.

Camp 2 is well positioned to climb from. It is poorly positioned to be comfortable or sleep in, as it is just too high. It sits at the base of the Southwest Face and the sun doesn't rise until late over the ridge of Everest. The tents are perched on shaky and uneven rock platforms. Food is hard to digest. It is cold, it is miserable, it is all you would expect from Everest.

But we didn't want to go down, down, all the way to Base Camp. Up here at Camp 2 we would be in position, our minds would be pulled upward, we would not be comfortable enough to give up and just go back to bed. So we pulled in new weather reports, we snacked on cheese and crackers and lived on noodles. At least I did, freeze-dried food being something I'd given up long ago. I ate dinner with the Sherpas, dal bhat and tsampa pancakes. It was all carbs, easy to digest, and the company was good. The Sherpas were working; it was just another day. I was working I reminded myself; hang in there. Hanging on Everest and being comfortable with it is essential. But Camp 2 was brutal, too much time, too long nights, too little air.

Was I to fail yet again? I lay in my tent. Long afternoons, winds annoyingly flapping the tent. Snow echoing out of the clouds. I was hungry and didn't want to eat. Tired and didn't want to sleep. Behind camp the Southwest Face rose up to the summit and winds ripped across the ridge like a train barrelling down from the heights. You can look straight up from Camp 2 and see the South Summit, the Summit Ridge and the summit. In clouds and wreathed in the jet stream, it looks another world, an unobtainable world. Would we be able to climb again, having been up to nearly the Balcony, 8400 metres (27,559 feet), then back down for a few nights of supposed rest at Camp 2, then back up to Camp 3, back up to the South Col and then back to the top? Would the season give us another chance, or was it a season when winter faded, and the summit window had opened and shut with no second chance? Impatience levels on Everest, the desire once in the thick of it to get up, get out and go home, were rising by the minute. And I was guiding, I reminded myself. I was supposed to be cheery and happy and motivating. I was doing my best.

Three days later the forecast improved. Back up, on to the endless ropes of the Lhotse Face, the mountain now much cleared of people. It had been a long season, and many had packed up and gone home. Others had gone high as we had on our first attempt, and had no power left, no stamina. And some teams didn't have the strong Sherpas, the oxygen supplies and the support to really stick it out and make another attempt. It was sad, but it was very good for us as round two would be done with fewer inexperienced climbers clogging the lines and poorly organised groups in the mix. Perhaps this time we could find some enjoyment in the heights?

The ice was beaten into steps on the Lhotse Face from the many climbers who had gone up and down, a welcome respite on the brick-hard ice. Camp 3, a hellish spot at best, was tipping off the mountain, the tents melting out and sliding down the hill. We put in new tent stakes and passed a fast night, sipping oxygen. At dawn we were off again, winds dropping and heat rising; it was soon too hot. The first time to the South Col I'd climbed up without oxygen. This time I turned on the air and four hours later was at the Col. Oxygen did have its advantages.

David Hamilton and I shared a tent, commiserating, planning, wandering out to dive into our teammates' tents and make sure everyone was ready. The forecast was good again, perhaps it would work? Neither David nor I had been to the top, so there was a mix of helping others coupled with a very large dose of personal enthusiasm. I'd had a farewell before I'd left at The Explorers Club in New York in front of the 1400 attendees, joining Peter Hillary and Jamling Tenzing Norgay on stage to receive a flag for our climb. Everest's fiftieth anniversary was anything but a quiet affair. I called down to Base Camp that evening from the South Col: 'Hey Robert, I have someone who wants to talk to you.'

'Robert, hi, it's Peter, we just got to Base Camp. How's the weather up there?'

Peter Hillary had climbed the mountain for the second time the year before with National Geographic and returned this year leading a trek. We had hoped to meet up in Base Camp, but just talking to him from the South Col before our second summit attempt seemed fortuitous.

'You'll be fine, Robert,' Peter encouraged me. 'The forecast looks good and you already know the way.' I'd almost forgotten about my climb to the South Summit with Ed and Stephen so long ago. Peter was right, I thought, I just needed to keep going, to do that last ridge. I'd been so close. I had a strong team and great Sherpas and we had all the oxygen we could need. What could possibly go wrong? But it was Everest. Had I perhaps used up my nine lives?

I went around the tents again, checking on the team. Everyone was good, rested, well fed and sipping oxygen.

I talked with Sibusiso. 'Are you going to the top this time, Robert? All the way to the top?'

'Yes,' I reassured him, perhaps with more confidence than anyone can really feel. 'The top, all the way to the top.'

'Okay,' Sibu said, 'I'll go with you.'

When we started for the top that night, Sibu would never be more than a metre behind or in front of me all the way up. From being an African bush guide to a Himalayan mountaineer, he was one of the fastest learners, the fittest and most talented climbers I'd climbed with. Our Sherpas loved him; I could hear them in their dining tent late at night in Base Camp talking and laughing together.

In the icefall the first time, I'd been with Sibu, attempting to take him from a crampon beginner to expert in a day or less. My patience levels were not all they could have been. At the football field in the midst of the Khumbu Icefall we paused for a rest and I asked Sibu how he was doing. 'Good,' he replied. A pause and then, 'You see that ice tower up there, that big one, it looks like a lion I know well in the park. The same shape.'

Here we were in the depths of the icefall and Sibu was pointing out lion shapes. It was a very good thing, the ability to climb and interact and appreciate the mountain at the same time. His crampon technique may have left much to be desired at first, but his appreciation of the mountain was strong. He had the best attitude and was always fun to climb with, more than I could say about myself at times.

This time as we climbed off the South Col towards the summit the weather held, the route played out below us, we switched out our oxygen tanks at the Balcony and stomped up the ridge, suspended between Nepal on our left and Tibet on our right. Our previous foray had tired us marginally, but the extra altitude time and knowing the start of the route made the climb familiar and I felt stronger. Because the number of other climbers had dropped dramatically, we could actually climb, moving up the ropes as we wished, out onto the crest of the ridge and up onto the South Summit as the sun rose. We were finally able to feel like we were really climbing Everest.

As Peter Hillary had reminded me, I'd been here fifteen years before, in a white-out, finishing off the Kangshung Face on my climb up the final ridge with Ed and Stephen. But that time I couldn't see, and in the end there was no choice, I couldn't even tell which way was up. I still remembered thinking then, 'Well, I must just come back then.' As if it was something I'd do the next day, or perhaps a week later.

Now, fifteen years later, I had the weather, I had oxygen, and I had the team around me to climb with. David Hamilton and I had met in Kathmandu for the first time, and I quickly realised how similar our approach to climbing and guiding was. By the time we started climbing, there was little we had to discuss and we didn't have a disagreement in two months of working together — we simply made decisions and led the team up the hill. David had been in high mountains and guiding for years, his experience and decision making took in the myriad of inputs and he made the right decisions quickly and naturally. At the South Summit we changed out our oxygen bottles for the Summit Ridge.

From the South Summit, the final ridge is a phenomenal ice and rock cacophony, slicing across the heavens. Just after dawn the intense rays of sun hit the Kangshung Face and illuminated it in a yellow glowing orb below, falling away four vertical kilometres into the Kama Valley. I could look down and feel every step of our Kangshung Face route below, seeing the long slope heading down to our Camp 2, then the rolling slopes heading out to Camp 1 before the face dropped away and out of view. Then the glacier appeared and the tongue of rocky moraine where we had put our Advanced Base Camp came into view, the camp I had virtually crawled back into after coming so near to dying on the Kangshung Face. The Kama Valley was a hazy Shangri La so far below, hovering, a different world.

The Southeast Ridge of Everest from the South Summit, just after sunrise, on a perfect day to climb unencumbered to the top of the world.
Photo: Robert Anderson

The winter clarity, the cold air, the North Face from the Pang La Pass, Tibet.

*Everest summit shadow suspended in the horizon looking
west from the South Summit, over the summit of Nuptse.*
Photo: Robert Anderson

For explorers like Stephen Venables and Robert Anderson, a reliable timepiece is more than a convenience; it's a necessity. Braving the remote heights of Mount Everest without

the aid of bottled oxygen, they needed to time their ascent with extreme caution. Their

The Twinlock winding crown protects movement from the elements

goal was to reach camp before sunset, when high winds and poor visibility make the mountain even more

They faced Everest without oxygen. But not without Rolex.

perilous. The timepiece they depended on was Rolex.

Part of what makes a Rolex Oyster so dependable is the design of its rugged case, which is hewn from a solid block of metal, using up to sixty tons of pressure.

To the Oyster case, we add the Twinlock winding crown. Designed according to the same principle as a submarine hatch, the Twinlock keeps dust and moisture from reaching the movement. One of the final additions to the case is the scratch-resistant synthetic sapphire crystal. Together, the case, winding crown and crystal protect the Rolex movement under even the most adverse conditions.

After undergoing a series of grueling tests at Rolex, Oyster

Every Oyster case is hewn from a solid ingot of stainless steel, 18kt gold or platinum.

timepieces are sent to an independent Swiss Institute, the Contrôle Officiel Suisse des Chronomètres. There, each watch must successfully undergo fifteen days and nights of rigorous testing before it is awarded the prestigious red seal that signifies it is an Official Swiss Chronometer. The extraordinary process that goes into making a Rolex helps explain why explorers find it valuable in any environment, from the frozen icescapes of the Arctic to the burning deserts of the Sahara. While there are many things explorers may need, a Rolex timepiece is one thing they can't do without.

Only officially certified Swiss Chronometers carry this seal.

ROLEX

Rolex Oyster Perpetual Explorer II in stainless steel with matching Oyster bracelet.
Write for brochure. Rolex Watch U.S.A., Inc., Dept. RLX, Rolex Building. 665 Fifth Avenue, New York, N.Y. 10022 5383.
Rolex, ♔, Oyster Perpetual, Explorer II, Twinlock and Oyster are trademarks

Rolex, my now seemingly lifelong sponsor, has featured from the first Everest expedition I led, for all my Seven Summits Solo expeditions and the reunion dinners and talks with my teams when we met together at The Explorers Club, New York City; the Royal Geographic Society, London; and the Smithsonian, Washington DC.

"While standing on top of Everest,
I looked across the valley, towards the other
great peak, Makalu, and mentally worked out
a route about how it could be climbed . . .

it showed me that, even though I was
standing on top of the world,
it wasn't the end of everything for me,
by any means.

I was still looking beyond
to other interesting challenges."

Sir Edmund Hillary

Everest (top) and Makalu, seem from over 8000 metres on the other peak, almost exactly a year apart. With my favourite quote from Sir Edmund Hillary on his first ascent.
Photo: Robert Anderson

Sunrise from Everest Southeast Ridge, the best dawn of all on a clear day with the summit an hour away.
Photo: Robert Anderson

A unique view of Everest (right) from Makalu, under its afternoon plume. The South Col just visible through the clouds (centre), and Lhotse, the worlds' fourth highest peak on the left. Taken on the descent from the summit of Makalu, 20 kilometres to the east.
Photo: Robert Anderson

Everest North Face routes, from the far right profile of the West Ridge that I first climbed on in 1985, to the Super Couloir in 1990, along to the Great Couloir which I soloed up to 8410 metres, over to the Anderson Couloir leading to the North Ridge. Photo: Ed Webster, taken on his solo ascent of Changtse.

Peering around the South Summit of Everest on the descent. Makalu, the worlds' fifth highest peak in the background.
Photo: Robert Anderson

The author (left) and Peter Hillary on the summit of Carstensz Pyramid of Indonesia.
Photo: Alex Hillary

We dropped the 10 metres off the South Summit, and following a shoestring of a rope, climbed along the crest of the ridge to the base of the Hillary Step. As much as it had been climbed 50 years before, as much as it was festooned with frayed ropes, it still had a frightening aura, a sense of 'Can you do this?' attached to it.

Before doing the Kangshung Face, Ed Hillary had told me if I got that high, I would find it 'enjoyable, the last real climbing' on the route. But that was Ed Hillary talking, and standing at the base in reality, black rock above and the snow ridge suddenly cutting in next to it and framing the right side, it was intimidating. Yet the moves were fun, simple stems, a few steps up, then moving left — I unclipped from the tangle of ropes and simply climbed over them and out around the corner, with Sibusiso right behind me and David following along. We were early enough that few were in front of us and no one was coming down. After the step, the snow rolled up and then flattened out above the Summit Ridge cornice, a simple step, after step, after step.

Then the summit, that joyous, amazing place. Dancing alone on the summit, striding from side to side, the highest person in the world.

Now this, now back to going down. Because this time the real summit of Everest and this last life would be used getting down, not getting up.

Fred Ziel and I had turned from up to down, reclipped into the shoestring of the fixed rope that marked the Summit Ridge, and took a few steps.

Only then did I fully realise Fred couldn't actually see where to go. His steps took no account of the slope. He just extended his legs, put his feet out and rocked forward until they hit the snow and then repeated that with the other leg. Fred's 8000-metre peak experience included K2, Broad Peak, Cho Oyu, Manaslu and Shishapangma, high mountain time that was now serving him well. He had served what David Breashears had long ago called 'The Apprenticeship', the hard rock, steep ice and mountain time that makes great climbers. It was the ability to intuitively react to dangerous situations, to make the right decisions. And in this instance, to descend virtually from the summit of Everest to the South Col without being able to see properly.

I hadn't really realised how much the Summit Ridge twisted and turned on my climb up. We had just been focused on keeping moving, keeping marginally warm, and finally getting to the top. The very apex of the ridge and our route along it balanced between the Southwest Face and the Kangshung Face. It was spectacularly exposed, yet wasn't so hard, if you could see.

As we started down, the snow was even, we walked along. David Hamilton came up behind with Sibu and we went along together. But it was slow. Very slow. We had climbed up faster than this. Then the ridge twisted and the trail went to the lip of Tibet, a 4-kilometre drop-off down the Kangshung. Not the place you wanted to step, so I went behind and David went in front, placing Fred's feet and calling out to him:

'Left, left, more left!'

'Now right.'

'Big step.'

'Left again.'

It was too slow to even think about.

We struggled along to the top of the Hillary Step. There was a maze of ropes. Faded, twisted, appearing out of the snow at the top and then disappearing again. Other climbers passed us going down. At altitude the mind just picks up snippets, vivid bits of moments, then discards them. Like a dream.

David and I were both above Fred. Clipping him in, getting the rappel off the steep step set up. Fred had done so many rappels in his life it was actually easy. Just put your feet wide apart and go down backwards, taking little steps. He didn't even have to look over his shoulder.

David leaned over to me as Fred set off down, and said,

'I don't think he is going to make it,' then he too rappelled.

'Oh no,' I thought. 'Not that.' Not, 'not making it'. In the fog of altitude, of cold, of toes numb and body weary and just wanting to go down, down, down, I didn't want any of this 'not making it'. Fred had to make it because I was his guide and I had to make it down with him. Here I was, first time to the top, first time guiding Everest. I had made it up. Now we had to make it down. Guiding was about we, not me. I knew I wasn't going down without Fred.

David, Fred and I huddled together again at the bottom of the Hillary Step. David put a short rope on Fred, and we led him across the path to the base of the South Summit.

This is where Rob Hall had huddled with Doug Hansen. All night. Then on his final call to his wife: 'I love you. Sleep well, my sweetheart. Please don't worry too much.'

Rob then spent another night and at some point he died. I still have the postcard Rob had sent me from Base Camp before they left for the top. I wanted none of that going on, that sense of being sucked into Everest and never coming back.

Huddling below the South Summit, and it being in the shade of late morning already, wasn't a good place. We clambered up and out. I went first, David put Fred's crampons in the footsteps from behind and we soon came out on top of the South Summit. We sent Sibu ahead; he was strong, he was fast, he didn't need to hang around for hours and this was David's and my job, helping people up, getting them down. We were in for whatever it took.

Now it was just down, all down, just a very long way. David and I got Fred's goggles cleaned up and on his face. His oxygen was gone, not helping anything, but we had no more spare bottles so I took mine off and switched it over. 'What do I care?' I thought. I'd been this high before without oxygen. All we had to do was go down, and Fred undoubtedly needed it more than me. Five minutes later, I felt my vision tunnel in and I had to consciously start breathing like an animal. Huffing and puffing. There was nothing heroic about Everest now.

The fixed ropes leading off the South Summit were a maze. We unclipped Fred and tied on a short rope. David and I alternated going in front and in back. Passang, our lone Sherpa still with us, had been climbing with Fred and had followed us down from the top and was helping out. With Passang and David behind Fred and me shouting directions from the front and putting his feet in place on the big steps, we kept moving.

I'd hoped some of Fred's vision would return. The 'I can't see' would become 'I can see better now'. When I checked it was just a muttered 'not so bright any more'.

Yet it seemed better for a while, as the slope remained consistent and we kept moving, Fred was picking up some details, at least able to see where we were on the mountain and in relation to the peaks around us. We had no water, we had frozen Snickers chocolate bars, which were inedible. Then the midday clouds, the winds, the inevitable afternoon storm, started lifting and brewing up from below. If a storm came in as it had in 1996 when eleven people had died, things would get very ugly. And we were getting slower and slower, everyone going down had now passed us; we were very much alone on the heights of Everest.

David too felt like we should have made it quite a long way down by now. Then his oxygen ran out as well, having lasted little longer than mine. He checked the altitude; 8600 metres (28,215 feet). We were now deep into what is fashionably called the death zone, without oxygen, and moving like snails.

'Oh well,' David said to himself, 'This is no different than descending from the same height as the summit of K2 with no bottled oxygen.' Nothing like a bit of optimism as your head starts to pound and your vision tunnels from lack of air.

We were suspended somewhere between the South Summit and the Balcony, a snowy shelf that never got any closer. We just kept going down, occasionally sitting down. Fred just seemed to get better and better at feeling his way down the slope and David and Passang went ahead while I stayed behind, clutching the rope and shouting 'Left, right, left.' And 'Big step, small step.' And whenever he paused, 'Another step, another step,' with bated impatience.

Across the South Col, Lhotse still hovered below us for the longest time. I would think, 'We have gone down a long way, we are getting down, we are getting closer.' Then I'd look out at Lhotse through the afternoon cloud and it would still be down there, far below us, and I'd realise we had barely moved. Snow misted out of the clouds around us. 'Would there be a storm?' We had no choice; less thought was better than any thought. Just keep moving down.

Above the Balcony the slope eased, but snow ridges and miniature cornices welled up. I was impatient and went ahead of Fred. He was making it; he was doing well. We were making it, really making it down.

Then I spaced out that Fred really couldn't see, went around a big dip in the ridge, stepping right and then left. He didn't step right or left, just put his foot out into space and toppled and rolled down into a dip in the ridge, tumbling head over foot until he stopped. 'Oh no,' I thought. It was 5 metres of rolling and tumbling he didn't need. I went over and helped him up. Headed in the right direction. The afternoon was fading away quickly.

'You have to tell me where to go. I can't see,' Fred reminded me.

Fred had been remarkably stoic. He hadn't complained. He hadn't voiced any worry. He just kept going down. I was quite astounded as once we had the oxygen on him and got lower, even as the hours passed, he just kept moving, kept taking cautious step after cautious step. I couldn't imagine what he was thinking, unseeing on Everest. Somewhere inside there was a real hero. Meanwhile, I was approaching that sense of tiredness where your body just wants to escape, is screaming to escape — and I could see. I was worried about the dark, then reminded myself it would matter little to Fred. It was just David, Passang and I, and we just needed to turn on our headlamps.

Finally, Fred and I reached the Balcony and David and Passang were there with a new oxygen bottle for Fred. There didn't seem to be any more for David and me. We'd given up on it, having gone this far; it seemed of little relevance.

'Maybe we should stay here?' I ventured to Fred. 'Maybe rest? Just go down tomorrow?' It was still a long way at our pace to the Col. The sun was falling rapidly towards the horizon. It would be dark soon.

'No way,' said Fred stridently. 'We go down. We are not staying here.'

Fred had a natural mountain sense honed by intuition — he inherently knew staying high just wasn't an option we wanted to take. And as much as we had been with him so far, would we take this opportunity to leave him? David and I certainly weren't going anywhere; we were in this until the end. But the numerous tales of people being left high on the mountain, of people sitting and waiting and dying as others passed them, seemed to happen every season now.

Okay, so we go down. Fred wanted to go down, knew instinctively he needed to go down now. So we went down. It was completely empty on the mountain now, we were totally alone, everyone else back at the South Col.

I got in front of Fred, and on the steeper slopes leading off the Balcony, David and Passang were behind, holding tight. It was the tougher job, holding Fred back, almost sliding him down the hill in places. I was still shouting 'Left, right' and getting the feet in the footsteps. David and Passang were the brakes. If the brakes failed, I'd have Fred's crampons in my face.

The afternoon storm had luckily been just that, an afternoon storm. Blowing in, swirling up, blowing away. Thankfully and luckily. The sun streamed through the clouds, Everest up high is a different beast, removed from reality and from life below. Dying would be very easy up here. It wouldn't really make that much difference, which could be why so many people do it. And now it was going to get dark.

'I have to go down, I really have to go down,' said Passang.

He had been with us all day. He was on his first summit and, more importantly, his first descent from Everest. At eighteen, the joys of high-altitude guiding were not yet ingrained. And so Passang disappeared down and it was David and me alone with Fred. We pulled out our headlamps. David stayed on the tail end of the rope, holding on.

I placed Fred's feet and kept calling directions. If I thought directions weren't needed, I'd pause. Then Fred would pause. He really didn't know where to go. My body was weary to the core. I realised the no-oxygen descent wasn't helping, though the air was thickening up. Simple thoughts of water or food were long gone. My body felt like a shell carrying a few random body parts along within it. It was just down, and down, and down.

Far below the occasional headlamp from the South Col flashed up at us. They were tiny darts of light, fireflies on the mountain. I was so weary now, and the slope finally started to ease. 'I'll go ahead,' I told David. 'I'll find the next rope.'

As the slope lessened the fixed rope ended, not at a knot, not at an anchor, just classic Everest style, it ended in the middle of the slope, just flopping about on the snow. But we weren't down, not even close really at the pace we were now going. There was a terrace, and then waves of ice crashing down below us, miniature crevasses and steep sloping steps that led for another few hundred metres down to the South Col camp. The sky was black with lots of stars. When I left the top rope the lights of the South Col faded behind the rise before the ice dropped off again. The wind howled and gusted in the dark as the air chilled. The night before when we had started for the summit, we had simply followed the line of lights up and across the slope. There was nothing to aim for on our way down.

I struck out across the slope, suddenly lost and only knowing I had to find a lone anchor in the dark and buried in the snow where the lower rope started. Without that rope we would be stuck on the terrace above the South Col Camp for the night. I used every thought I could find, traversing right and then left. No rope appeared in my headlight beam, no lone snow stake sticking from the snow. Suddenly, I saw another light coming up towards me. A body appeared below it, climbing up and across the slope, with weary steps.

'Robert, Robert, I can't find the rope.'

It was Passang. He had left us two hours before, disappeared down the mountain and now was lost in the dark and had been wandering around looking for the rope to get him back to camp.

I sat down in the snow. This was bad. We didn't want to spend the night out. As much as I knew we would make it, it wouldn't be fun. I'd bivouacked without oxygen above the South Col with Ed and Stephen after climbing the Kangshung Face. I'd curled up in snow holes alone on the North Face. But we really needed to be down and in a bed or the South Col equivalent.

I couldn't find the rope down with logic or tracking back and forth. I needed somehow to just get a sense of where to go, to feel it. I could see David's headlamp closing up behind me as they descended off the last rope. I remembered how we had angled across from the end of one rope to the other. I stood up and simply let my intuition guide me, not trying to reason it out, not trying to think, just feeling the slope and the mountain, taking eighteen years of climbing on Everest, much of it in the dark, and hoping at least I'd internalised something and the intuition I'd had on my first expedition held through until this last one.

When I saw the rope in my feeble headlamp beam, it was even smaller and less visible than I thought it would be. A subtle glow of the aluminium stake, a white twisted rope appearing out of the snow and leading off into the dark below.

'I got it,' I shouted back up to Passang. He came across. He pulled the rope from the snow tiredly and clipped into it, clutching the lifeline that would lead him down.

'Go ahead,' I said. 'I'll wait,' and waved my arm back up the hill at David and Fred. Passang disappeared rapidly down the rope, crampons crunching the ice. David came down, Fred just in front. He had no headlamp and it made no difference. We clipped Fred in and David shepherded him down.

Now we had the last rope, I knew we were down. I was suddenly desperate to be finished, to lie down, to not move. I wanted to be in my own tent and not think and to drink warm water. It already felt like we had been up all night, all of a second night in reality. I slid down a few ropes over the twisted ice, sculpted and twisted by the wind, until the South Col's dark tent shapes appeared below in the gloom. I moved off in front of Fred and David; they would be fine now. I had to get to my tent.

I had no power left in my body; my mind was just moving me along. The ice eased and the flat scree of the Col reached my boots, crampons clanging around on the rocks. I could see the rough tent outlines. They flapped. Where was my tent? All I wanted was my tent. Where could it be?

I heard a muffled shout from a tent close by. 'Robert, Robert, is that you?' Alejandro, another on my team. 'Robert, come over here.'

I stumbled across.

'Your tent blew down. But don't worry, we have your things, and your sleeping bag, it is all here and all ready, come in.'

The tent I'd been dreaming of all day was gone, that moment of crawling in and finally collapsing, of lying flat on the earth and unmoving was all shattered.

But Alejandro and Rodrigo were ready, welcoming in that solicitous and caring way of Latin countries. They pulled me into the tent, passed over hot water, added in another bottle and got me out of my down suit and into my sleeping bag.

'We will massage your feet,' and before I could complain they also had my socks off and were rubbing my feet.

'It's important, it's good. Then you can sleep.'

I lay half comatose. We had left at 8 p.m. the night before. It was now after 11 p.m.

Twenty-seven hours, that was a long summit climb.

I lay in the tent unable to move, just listening, waiting. I wasn't really down until we were all down.

The crunch of crampons on the rock. David's voice. Our Dutch teammate Kiek pulled him and Fred into his tent. The water was ready, their sleeping bags also laid out, we were well looked after.

I really felt like I had finally used up all of my nine lives.

I'd climbed Everest, finally. I was too tired to feel much beyond relief right now. But the knowing, the sense of knowing the mountain that I had wanted so badly, of feeling every step up to the top of the world, was fulfilled. And, more importantly, the team was all back and safe, or at least as safe as you can be at 8000 metres in a tiny tent on Everest. And I was still alive, barely it seemed. But alive.

I'd never read anything about the climb down from the South Col of Everest. It was always, 'then we went down'. I wanted to enjoy it, to feel the release of gravity and the filling of the air again into the lungs, the thoughts clearing and the muscles returning.

We had more Sherpas at the South Col to help, and by morning Fred had hazy vision, enough to allow him to head down without guidance on every step.

Fred would come back a few years later to the north side of Everest, to make another attempt in 2005 and then finally to return and summit in 2007. His need to ring the summit bell, to validate his mountaineering skills and finish it all with a magical and fulfilling experience. He finished off those last few metres to the summit and was able to look over the top and see his high point on the south side when he had been oh so close to the top of the world with us four long years before.

We all left the South Col together and climbed out over the Geneva Spur, dropping in a long and drooping rappel down the rock and into the snow. Over the Yellow Band, sliding past Camp 3 and then rappel after rappel after rappel down the Lhotse Face. It was like rappelling Yosemite's El Cap, starting in the clouds with the ground miles below, then infinite rappels and then looking down and seemingly being no closer.

Camp 2 was finally comfortable, a good sleep, a call on the phone for a ride on the helicopter from Base Camp two days hence to get us home quickly. We were out of here. In Camp 2 again, David and I rested up quickly, Fred's vision rapidly recovered and Sibu was in high spirits as ever.

Everest never gives up, though. Never. As we descended the icefall, a trail of red droplets soon appeared, a trail of life left and weeping out from a body bag of an Indian climber who had fallen in a crevasse the day before. Getting through the icefall is difficult at the best of times, towing a body bag through it took a small army of Indian teammates and Sherpas to accomplish. In the heat, the body unfroze and the blood trail was soon an endless red line alongside the fixed rope.

As we waited behind the body train, the helicopter we had booked for the following day, an immense grey Russian behemoth with a large smiling glass window under the cockpit, thundered up the Khumbu Glacier and hovered down over the edge of Base Camp as it prepared to land. Then it tipped, overcorrected and plummeted straight down with a resounding crash into the glacier. Blades shattered and ricocheted off the rocks. Ice shattered below it and the helicopter rolled onto its side. We were still an hour above Base Camp but could see people rushing bug-like over to the chopper. Two more people would die, the fractured and ricocheting helicopter blade whirring off onto the trail and into two trekkers.

We finally passed the Indian climber's body at a ladder, the Sherpas and Indian team waving us past. The fatigue, the body, the chopper falling from the sky, fatigue now welling up from the long summit night and the heat from the reflecting sun surrounded us at the base of the icefall.

I sat down on a rock and slowly unclipped my crampons. A Sherpa poured tea.

Eighteen years, nine expeditions to Everest. It had truly been nine lives. And then some.

EPILOGUE:
EVEREST SOUTH COL –
LIFE IS KNOWING

Nine expeditions to Everest. Nine lives well and truly used up.

Was there any reason to ever go back? Wasn't the obsession complete?

Everest had taken a lot, but I felt what it gave back was far greater. I'd never been more alive, had more fun, nor admittedly been as close to death so often as on Everest.

There was nothing like an Everest expedition. The intensity, the atmosphere, the heights, the history and the climbers. It wrapped all the human emotions up into a tightly wound ball and played them out in a condensed time frame. You live a whole life in two months.

As much as had been written about the deaths, the garbage, the lack of ethics and the easy climbing that no self-respecting real climber would be interested in, Everest, if you wanted to look a bit closer, was a very fine climb. The South Col route was superb, from having to brave the icefall, to walking through the Western Cwm, the immense 'Valley of Silence'. Then testing yourself on the Lhotse Face and finishing on what must surely be the finest ridge climb in the world, leading to the actual top of the world.

There is no better place to see the sunrise than from the South Summit of Everest with the top of the world rising just in front of you.

By 2010, David Hamilton was well into his eventual ten successful summits guiding climbers to the top. But he decided to take a year off.

And, again, came a short email, very short, from Simon Lowe at Jagged Globe:

'Everest perhaps then?'

If I timed it right, I could take another hiatus from advertising, take time off for Everest, fit in Cho Oyu in the autumn of the same year, and with thoughts of Makalu already being discussed for the next year, tackle what I thought was the most beautiful peak in the Himalayas the next spring. Leading teams on three 8000-metre peaks over the next year and a half had far more appeal than another year at a desk, no matter how much they wanted to pay me.

So off I went again. This time I wanted to expend no more lives and perhaps enjoy the climb more. Was that possible? Much depended on the team, and in that respect I was to be singularly blessed.

Tim had done six of the seven summits. 'No, not Everest,' he wisely thought, 'I don't need that.' So he had gone to climb neighbouring Ama Dablam in the autumn instead. When he reached the top, he looked out over the jagged ridge of Nuptse, across that framing, sweeping curve of the blackness of the Lhotse Face and there sat Everest. And he realised, 'Yes, I need to go climb Everest.'

Angus Ruddle was with him on Ama Dablam, and in Angus fashion, he said, 'Maybe I will go with you.' So he did. He worked on people's hearts, he knew about blood and oxygen and about not having enough heart. Angus had plenty of heart.

And Bunter Anson had just been up Manaslu. Bunter was so understated you wouldn't expect to find him on Everest. There are a lot of egos on 8000-metre peaks, but Bunter was happy to just climb, to enjoy, to mix a late-night laugh with an early morning Lhotse Face. On Everest, the ability to smile at 2 a.m., when the moon is bright and the ice is sharp, is probably one of the best qualifiers for success.

There were also, of course, the Brothers Grimm. Not really, though Ruairidh Finlayson was certainly more serious about the climb. His brother Foo had gotten them started on the Seven Summits and into all this trouble in the first place. Foo had a rather nonchalant approach: 'I admit to not really training for this,' he confessed at the top of the icefall. We were out in front and his lack of training wasn't at all evident. Fortunately, it was balanced by an efficiency of movement and a rare talent that more than covered him. They were not possessed of brotherly love down low, but up high they were as close as brothers can be. And not to foreshadow, but they certainly did know how to climb. With that natural, 'this is a pain, this is dangerous, but I'm having a good time anyway' sensibility that is so important in getting to the top of the world.

And Michael, 'Where are your crampons?' Michael. Long before an expedition starts, a guide gets medical forms, climbing forms, 'what I want to be when I grow up' forms. And then there is a rental section. Do you want a sleeping bag, an ice axe, maybe some crampons?

When you climb Everest, you normally have crampons, usually four pairs or more, and you pick two and bring them both. The twelve points a foot connect you to the mountain through the good, bad and ugly and you wear them the entire way from Base Camp to the Summit. Not owning a pair or two is highly suspect. Yet Michael had rented his crampons. It was a worry. I asked him about this on our trek in.

'I don't want to take this too seriously,' he said. 'These mountains are high and dangerous; I don't want to get too committed.' He had rented crampons and successfully stomped up another 8000-metre peak, Manaslu, so why buy them?

And Tore Rasmussen had been up the North Side of Everest already, and thought maybe the South Side of Everest would be good to climb too. Why not? After all, no Norwegian had done that.

That was our team. If you looked for homogeneity, for a puzzle piece of humanity climbing Everest, you wouldn't find it here. More than anything else, that made guiding Everest and going back for yet another climb the most interesting profession on earth: taking people from all climbs of life and seeing if I could help them along their way to 'the top of the world'. There was, however, one constant: we were all dreamers. And probably dangerous — as T.E. Lawrence said:

> All men dream, but not equally. Those who dream by night in the dusty recesses of their minds, wake in the day to find that it was vanity: but the dreamers of the day are dangerous men, for they may act on their dreams with open eyes, to make them possible.

Tore, Angus, Ruairidh and Foo were fit, impatient and we found a day of good weather and they charged onward and upward. Up, and up, and up, they went. We saw them again on the way down.

They were wearing the Everest Smile.

The smile shines through fatigue and grime and sunburn and no sleep-in days and reflects reaching the top of the world. It was their happy hearts smiling and we took their picture and off they romped down the mountain. Now it was our turn. My fourth time camping on the South Col, but still a singular and frightening place with big winds and even bigger views.

As ever it is windy, airless, freezing. A few hours after arrival, we finish our noodles, cheese and crackers and get dressed (long underwear, fleece, down suit, liner socks, woolly socks, inner boots, outer boots, crampons, big gloves, pack on, oxygen on, mask on, eyes blurred — oh woe to having to go to the bathroom). At 8.30 p.m. we get to go climbing. It takes until I reach the Balcony four hours later to really establish a rhythm, then I get into gear. I'm up over 8400 metres at last, there is a hope of sunrise, I can go to work up here and the higher I go, the better I feel.

Michael was up in front, his rental crampons showing the way. He was tagging along with his ever-enthusiastic Sherpa Pemchiri. Tim and I climbed along behind them; Mingma, my Sherpa, had 'pains in his chest' in the night. Not a great thing at 8400 metres. We climb slower, we are both carrying an extra bottle of oxygen for the team and I don't want to lose him. Mingma rests, he wanders along behind me, then he slides his mask sideways and smiles and I know he feels better. Talk is superfluous above 8000 metres.

Tim is climbing along confidently and comfortably, we get hung up behind people who can't get over an overhanging step, a gasping, heaving, goggle-fogging black-rock bulge you have to lift your feet high on and haul yourself over. If you grew up climbing rocks, it isn't a problem, otherwise it is nothing less than desperate. Tim and I give him a push to speed things up and he flops up and over onto the ledge above.

Then we are up onto the final steep snow rib, the extreme Southeast Ridge, the rib to the sky. The sun, the oh where can it be sun, finally shimmers far out, black against Kanchenjunga, then illuminates the dark shadow of Makalu. The South Summit appears, a cornice formed by the jet stream, hanging from Nepal and extending far out over into Tibet, a cornice so big it takes up two countries. It extends far out over the Kangshung Face like a solid cloud of ice.

The chance to do this climb a second time, to climb it without the overwhelming focus on the summit, has created a much bigger experience, far bigger than my first climb. Tiptoeing on steel points across the ice to the summit is magical. The moves over the Hillary Step, how close to heaven one feels. To be able to anticipate the sensations makes it doubly worthwhile. There is a desire to summit but no longer a burning need. Hence there is more time to think, to look, to feel the ridge, pause for the view to sink in, rest in the thoughts and hold it there forever.

We dance along, around a final grey shattered buttress, scene of Fred's original highpoint, and then up and up. Then a last five steps, a swivel round and I am sitting again atop the top of the world.

The sky above is bigger than the earth below, more connected to heaven, whether you believe in it or not. The air, the oxygen, is forgotten. The importance of photos fades. The relief of reaching this singular place, the flood of being there, of attaining a rare absolute, is overwhelming. There are hugs and back slaps, there are men and women in tears. And for guides there is the sense we are in the earth's most dangerous place, the one closest to death, and it will be very nice to get down.

So down and down we go. The summit is in our legs, our toes warm, our water is gone, down and down; did we really come up all this way? This time it is fast, though, we are back at the South Col for lunch, a big lunch, and hide away in our tents to let the afternoon snowstorm blow through and the sun slip into the vale of Nepal. We have worked so hard to get here, now on our descent we can savour the heights with the summit behind us.

Two days later we take off the crampons at the base of the Khumbu Icefall, we shed the armour, the shells, the ego and ropes, and walk lighthearted to our Base Camp.

We have proved ourselves happy under deathly ice towers, we have persevered up the endless Lhotse Face and we showed faith in the darkness that led us to the top of the world.

We dreamed by night and by day and stepped into heaven at dawn. And, best of all, it was very nice to get back to earth with all our teammates, with my nine lives still intact.

ACKNOWLEDGEMENTS

This is a personal book about high altitude climbing, where facts, viewpoints and occasionally even the height we were at can differ. If I have made mistakes, they are all my own and apologies in advance should others remember it differently.

My eventual success on Everest, and staying alive along the way, was assisted in so many ways by many people and companies. With their support, encouragement and enthusiasm for my climbs I was able to not only undertake expeditions year after year but also share and perhaps inspire a much wider audience.

My success in completing this book is due to a good dose of encouragement from Josephine Clark, my partner in climbing and in life, who is now also my wife.

Endorsed Support and Lectures:
The American Alpine Club, American Geographical Society, The Explorers Club (flag #123), the American Himalayan Foundation,

Mount Everest Foundation, National Geographic Society, the Royal Geographic Society, the Smithsonian, United Nations.

Financial Support, Equipment and Services:

British Airways

Burroughs Wellcome

Chinese Mountaineering Association

Earth Sea Sky

FCB

Helly Hansen

Jagged Globe

Kiehl's since 1851

Kodak

Lowa Boots

Mountain Equipment

NBC

Nike

Ogilvy

Olympus

Opedix

Outdoor Research

Raynish & Partners

Rolex Watch

GSK

And thanks to my climbing partners and friends who have shared information, mountain time and maybe just pub time, including: Pete Athans, Conrad Anker, Bauer family, Steve Bell, Chris Bonington, David Breashears, Tom Briggs, Ann and John Clark, Wendy Davis, Rob Dorival, Mike Duncan, Phil Erard, Bob Guthrie, Intesar Haider, Chris and Laura Heintz, Hillary family, Roland and Helen Hunter, Harry Kent, Simon Lowe, Shane Lundgren, Nick Lydon, Reinhold Messner, Peggy Foster Miller, Passang Norbu, Martin Pazzani, Miklos Pinther, John

Roskelly, Andy Politz, Mike Perry, Schaefer family, Ying Dao Shui, Jay Smith, Hannah Szto, Norbu Tenzing, Richard Wallace, Eric Winkelman, Ed Viesturs, Dr Miriam Zieman.

With special thanks to Sandy Wylie for inspiring the book title, and edits and input on the manuscript from Josephine Clark, David Hamilton, Paul Teare, Stephen Venables, Sibusiso Vilane, Ed Webster and Dr Frederick Ziel.

And, finally, the many who inspired me in the mountains and whom I will always hold very fond memories of: Mads Anderson, Dick Bass, Mike Bearzi, Russell Belknap, Jim Bridwell, Hans Christian Doseth, Andy Fanshawe, Bill Forrest, Michael Gifkins, Tim Grainger, Randall Grandstaff, Dr Bill Hammel, Mark Hesse, Valery Khrichtchatyi, Xavi Lamas, Benoit Schaack, Fletcher Wilson.

THE EVEREST ROUTES
FROM *NINE LIVES*

West Ridge Direct — 1985

The West Ridge Direct is perhaps one of the longest, most convoluted, and varied routes on Everest. It was first attempted by a French team in 1974, when six died in an avalanche. Its first ascent was by a Yugoslavian team in 1979.

The actual West Ridge starts in Tibet and can be reached from the upper Central Rongbuk Glacier. But ascents traditionally start from Nepal, necessitating an additional 400 vertical metre climb from the Khumbu Glacier, straight up over the pass known as the Lho La leading into Tibet. From the Lho La, the route rises steeply up the ridge for 1000 metres, before making a very long traverse across to the base of the summit pyramid. The Direct route joins the traditional West Ridge route done by the Americans in 1963 along this traverse. That route then angles out onto the North Face and ascends the Hornbein Couloir. The Direct route goes straight up the final summit pyramid for another 1000 vertical metres to the top.

Pete Athans and I reached 8300 metres on our first summit attempt, before I went back with Jay Smith a few days later; climbing up to 8600 metres. Led by Dave Saas.

Kangshung Face — 1988

In 1983, an American team completed a long and challenging route on the central section of the Kangshung Face. The route I chose on the Kangshung was to the left, with my team including Paul Teare, Stephen Venables and Ed Webster, ascending a prominent rock buttress, and then the snow slopes leading directly up to the South Col. From the Col we followed Hillary and Tenzing's first ascent route to the summit. Well documented in both Stephen Venables' *Everest Kangshung Face* where Reinhold Messner commented 'You have done a very hard thing, but you were lucky,' and in Ed Webster's magnum opus, *Snow in the Kingdom.*

Stephen was the first British climber to summit Everest without oxygen, doing so on a new route and climbing alone above the South Col to the summit. Led by Robert Anderson.

Super Couloir — 1990

The Super Couloir, dominating the right side of Everest's North Face, was first climbed in its entirety by the Japanese in 1980. It connects the distinctive lower and broader couloir on the face to the upper section, completed by Hornbein and Unsoeld in 1963. The entire couloir was again ascended in 1986 by Loretan and Troillet in a single push without oxygen. Jay Smith, Mark Hesse, Harry Kent and I reached the centre of the North Face below the Hornbein Couloir at around 7700 metres. Led by Mark Hesse.

Anderson Couloir — 1991

Not a name for a publicised route until Ed Webster put together his magnificent chronology for *Ascent* magazine and kindly added it onto his route maps — and since he did, I'll keep it.

The couloir is a direct link from the upper Central Rongbuk Glacier, out onto the North Ridge at about 7500 metres. As you can ski up to 6700 metres on the glacier, it is an ideal high camp for the North Face and North Ridge, while still rarely visited and remote from the rest of Everest. I soloed up to 8100 metres on my first attempt, and later reached 8200 metres climbing with others on the North Ridge. Led by Robert Anderson.

North Ridge — 1992

A magnificent and natural line, first pioneered by the British in the 1920s, ascending to the North Col from the East Rongbuk Glacier and then continuing straight up to join the Northeast Ridge. A fun snow climb lower down followed by some even better scrambling up high, except for that rather tricky Second Step on summit day. A great off season or winter route (still not completed) which is heavily populated in the spring season. Paul Teare and I reached 8200 metres on our attempted climb from Advanced Base to the summit in a day. Led by Dan Larson.

Great Couloir — 1993

The entirety of the magnificent Great Couloir was first ascended by the Australian team led by Tim Macartney-Snape in 1984. Lincoln Hall's *White Limbo* was an inspiration for our own climb of the Kangshung Face four years later.

From the base of the North Face you can cut back under Changtse, with a long traverse on skis leading up to a basin right below the North Col. Camps can be made at 6500 metres or even tucked in under the North Face at 6700 metres. The route then joins the North Face proper and takes a long diagonal traverse leading to the upper half of the Great Couloir at 7600 metres. The Great Couloir is then ascended directly, through the Yellow Band and out onto the upper slopes of Everest. Mike Bearzi, Paul Teare and I reached the Couloir over multiple attempts, before I went back and soloed to 8410 metres. Led by Robert Anderson.

Great Couloir — 1995

Joined by Eric Winkelman, Mike Bearzi and I returned for a repeat attempt, reaching the base of the Couloir with Eric. On a subsequent attempt, Mike and I climbed up and camped out for two nights at 8100 metres high in the Couloir before being defeated by deep snow. Led by Robert Anderson.

North Ridge — Winter, 1999

Inspired by the opportunity to be either the last person up Everest of the century, or perhaps the first person up in the next, I obtained a rare winter permit from the Chinese Mountaineering Authority for the North Ridge. Stymied by cold, high winds and minimal infrastructure (all to be expected of course) I reached the North Col before retreating quickly to the relative warmth of New York to see in the New Year. As far as I know, no winter ascents have yet been made of Everest from Tibet.

South Col — 2003

The fiftieth anniversary ascent, up the traditional South Col route, with all the trappings, from a team of twelve, with a matching number of Sherpas, to several trekking groups and a BBC film crew. Summited 26 May with David Hamilton and Sibusiso Vilane. Led by Robert Anderson.

South Col — 2010

I returned to lead again for Jagged Globe on the South Col route, climbing with a strong team. Our first team led by Tore Rasmussen summited 17 May, with Ruairidh and Fionnlagh Finlayson and Angus Ruddle. On 23 May, I climbed to the Balcony with Bunter Anson and then went on to the summit with Mike Phethean and Tim Ralph. We climbed alongside and were of course very well supported by our strong Sherpa teammates who summited with us and included: Dawa Gyalze Sherpa, Mingma Sherpa, Mingma Tshering, Chhiri Sherpa and Pem Chhiri Sherpa. Led by Robert Anderson.

FEATURED CLIMBERS
AND PEOPLE